Bash Guide for Beginners

By Machtelt Garrels

Cover design by Fultus Books

ISBN 0-9744339-4-2

Published by Fultus Corporation
Corporate Web Site: www.fultus.com
Fultus eLibrary: elibrary.fultus.com
Online Book Superstore: store.fultus.com
email: production@fultus.com

Introduction

Why this book?

The primary reason for writing this book is that a lot of readers feel the existing HOWTO `<http://tldp.org/HOWTO/Bash-Prog-Intro-HOWTO.html>` to be too short and incomplete, while the Bash Scripting Guide `<http://tldp.org/LDP/abs/html/index.html>` is too much of a reference work. There is nothing in between these two extremes. I also wrote this book on the general principal that not enough inexpensive basic courses are available, though they should be.

This is a practical book which, while not always being too serious, tries to give real-life instead of theoretical examples. I partly wrote it because I don't get excited with stripped down and over-simplified examples written by people who know what they are talking about, showing some really cool Bash feature so much out of its context that you cannot ever use it in practical circumstances. You can read that sort of stuff after finishing this book, which contains exercises and examples that will help you survive in the real world.

From my experience as UNIX/Linux user, system administrator and trainer, I know that people can have years of daily interaction with their systems, without having the slightest knowledge of task automation. Thus they often think that UNIX is not userfriendly, and even worse, they get the impression that it is slow and old-fashioned. This problem is another one that can be remedied by this guide.

Who should read this book?

Everybody working on a UNIX or UNIX-like system who wants to make life easier on themselves, power users and sysadmins alike, can benefit from reading this book. Readers who already have a grasp of working the system using the command line will learn the ins and outs of shell scripting that ease execution of daily tasks. System administration relies a great deal on shell scripting; common tasks are often automated using simple scripts. This document is full of examples that will encourage you to write your own and that will inspire you to improve on existing scripts.

Prerequisites/not in this course:

- You should be an experienced UNIX or Linux user, familiar with basic commands, man pages and documentation
- Being able to use a text editor
- Understand system boot and shutdown processes, init and initscripts
- Create users and groups, set passwords
- Permissions, special modes
- Understand naming conventions for devices, partitioning, mounting/unmounting file systems
- Adding/removing software on your system

See Introduction to Linux `<http://tldp.org/LDP/intro-linux/html/index.html>` (or your local TLDP mirror `<http://www.tldp.org/mirrors.html>`) if you haven't mastered one or more of these topics. Additional information can be found in your system documentation (man and info pages), or at the Linux Documentation Project `<http://tldp.org>`.

Contributions

Thanks to all the friends who helped (or tried to) and to my husband; your encouraging words made this work possible. Thanks to all the people who submitted bug reports, examples and remarks - among many, many others:

- Hans Bol, one of the groupies
- Mike Sim, remarks on style
- Dan Richter, for array examples
- Gerg Ferguson, for ideas on the title
- Mendel Leo Cooper, for making room
- #linux.be, for keeping my feet on the ground

Special thanks to Tabatha Marshall, who volunteered to do a complete review and spell and grammar check. We make a great team: she works when I sleep. And vice versa.

Feedback

Missing information, missing links, missing characters? Mail it to the author: tille@coresequence.com

Don't forget to check with the latest version first: <http://tille.soti.org/training/bash/>

What do you need?

bash, available from <http://www.gnu.org/directory/GNU/>. The Bash shell is available on nearly every Linux system, and can these days be found on a wide variety of UNIX systems.

Compiles easily if you need to make your own, tested on a wide variety of UNIX, Linux, MS Windows and other systems.

Conventions used in this document

Table 1 describes the typographic and usage conventions that occur in this text.

Table 1: Typographic and usage conventions

Text type	Meaning
"Quoted text"	Quotes from people, quoted computer output.
terminal view	Literal computer input and output captured from the terminal, usually rendered in a box.
command	Name of a command that can be entered on the command line.
VARIABLE	Name of a variable or pointer to content of a variable, as in $VARNAME.
option	Option to a command, as in "the -a option to the **ls** command".
argument	Argument to a command, as in "read **man** *ls*".
command options arguments	Command synopsis or general usage, on a separated line.
filename	Name of a file or directory, for example "Change to the /usr/bin directory."
Key	Keys to hit on the keyboard, such as "type **Q** to quit".
Button	Graphical button to click, like the **OK** button.
Menu → Choice	Choice to select from a graphical menu, for instance: "Select **Help → About Mozilla** in your browser."
Terminology	Important term or concept: "The Linux *kernel* is the heart of the system."

\	The backslash in a terminal view or command synopsis indicates an unfinished line. In other words, if you see a long command that is cut into multiple lines, \ means "Don't press **Enter** yet!"
See Chapter 1, "Bash and Bash scripts"	link to related subject within this guide.
The author <http://tille.soti.org>	Clickable link to an external web resource.

The following images are used:

 This is a note. It contains additional information or remarks.

 This is a caution. It means be careful.

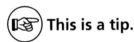 **This is a tip.**

Organization of this document

This guide discusses concepts useful in the daily life of the serious Bash user. While a basic knowledge of the usage of the shell is required, we start with a discussion of the basic shell components and practices in the first three chapters.

Chapters four to six are discussions of basic tools that are commonly used in shell scripts.

Chapters eight to twelve discuss the most common constructs in shell scripts.

All chapters come with exercises that will test your preparedness for the next chapter.

- Chapter 1, "Bash and Bash scripts": Bash basics: why Bash is so good, building blocks, first guidelines on developing good scripts.
- Chapter 2, "Writing and debugging scripts": Script basics: writing and debugging.
- Chapter 3, "The Bash environment": The Bash Environment: initialization files, variables, quoting characters, shell expansion order, aliases, options.

- Chapter 4, "Regular expressions": Regular expressions: an introduction.

- Chapter 5, "The GNU sed stream editor": Sed: an introduction to the sed line editor.

- Chapter 6, "The GNU awk programming language":Awk: introduction to the awk programming language.

- Chapter 7, "Conditional statements": Conditional statements: constructs used in Bash to test conditions.

- Chapter 8, "Writing interactive scripts": Interactive scripts: making scripts user-friendly, catching user input.

- Chapter 9, "Repetitive tasks": Executing commands repetitively: constructs used in Bash to automate command execution.

- Chapter 10, "More on variables": Advanced variables: specifying variable types, introduction to arrays of variables, operations on variables.

- Chapter 11, "Functions": Functions: an introduction.

- Chapter 12, "Catching signals": Catching signals: introduction to process signalling, trapping user-sent signals.

Contents

8   Writing interactive scripts   121

9   Repetitive tasks   139

10 More on variables   155

11 Functions   167

12 Catching signals   175

A Shell Features   181

Chapter 1

Bash and Bash scripts

In this introduction module we

- *Describe some common shells*
- *Point out GNU Bash advantages and features*
- *Describe the shell's building blocks*
- *Discuss Bash initialization files*
- *See how the shell executes commands*
- *Look into some simple script examples*

1.1 Common shell programs

The UNIX shell program interprets user commands, which are either directly entered by the user, or which can be read from a file called the shell script or shell program. Shell scripts are interpreted, not compiled. The shell reads commands from the script line per line and searches for those commands on the system (see Section 1.2), while a compiler converts a program into machine readable form, an executable file - which may then be used in a shell script.

Apart from passing commands to the kernel, the main task of a shell is providing a user environment, which can be configured individually using shell resource configuration files.

1.1.1 Shell types

Just like people know different languages and dialects, your UNIX system will usually offer a variety of shell types:

- **sh** or Bourne Shell: the original shell still used on UNIX systems and in UNIX-related environments. This is the basic shell, a small program with few features. While this is not the standard shell, it is still available on every Linux system for compatibility with UNIX programs.

- **bash** or Bourne Again shell: the standard GNU shell, intuitive and flexible. Probably most advisable for beginning users while being at the same time a powerful tool for the advanced and professional user. On Linux, **bash** is the standard shell for common users. This shell is a so-called *superset* of the Bourne shell, a set of add-ons and plug-ins. This means that the Bourne Again shell is compatible with the Bourne shell: commands that work in **sh**, also work in **bash**. However, the reverse is not always the case. All examples and exercises in this book use **bash**.

- **csh** or C shell: the syntax of this shell resembles that of the C programming language. Sometimes asked for by programmers.

- **tcsh** or Turbo C shell: a superset of the common C shell, enhancing user-friendliness and speed.

- **ksh** or the Korn shell: sometimes appreciated by people with a UNIX background. A superset of the Bourne shell; with standard configuration a nightmare for beginning users.

The file /etc/shells gives an overview of known shells on a Linux system:

```
mia:~> cat /etc/shells
/bin/bash
/bin/sh
/bin/tcsh
/bin/csh
```

Your default shell is set in the `/etc/passwd` file, like this line for user *mia*:

```
mia:L2NOfqdlPrHwE:504:504:Mia Maya:/home/mia:/bin/bash
```

To switch from one shell to another, just enter the name of the new shell in the active terminal. The system finds the directory where the name occurs using the PATH settings, and since a shell is an executable file (program), the current shell activates it and it gets executed. A new prompt is usually shown, because each shell has its typical appearance:

```
mia:~> tcsh
[mia@post21 ~]$
```

1.2 Advantages of the Bourne Again SHell

The GNU project (GNU's Not UNIX) provides tools for UNIX-like system administration which are free software and comply to UNIX standards.

Bash is an sh-compatible shell that incorporates useful features from the Korn shell (ksh) and C shell (csh). It is intended to conform to the IEEE POSIX P1003.2/ISO 9945.2 Shell and Tools standard. It offers functional improvements over sh for both programming and interactive use; these include command line editing, unlimited size command history, job control, shell functions and aliases, indexed arrays of unlimited size, and integer arithmetic in any base from two to sixty-four. Bash can run most sh scripts without modification.

Like the other GNU projects, the bash initiative was started to preserve, protect and promote the freedom to use, study, copy, modify and redistribute software. It is generally known that such conditions stimulate creativity. This was also the case with the bash program, which has a lot of extra features that other shells can't offer.

1.2.1 Invocation

In addition to the single-character shell command line options which can generally be configured using the **set** shell built-in command, there are several multi-character options that you can use. We will come across a couple of the more popular options in this and the following chapters; the complete list can be found in the Bash info pages, **Bash features → Invoking Bash**.

1.2.2   Bash startup files

Bash reads different startup files depending on how you invoke it.

Invoked as an interactive login shell, or with '–login'

Interactive means you can enter commands. The shell is not running because a script has been activated. A login shell means that you got the shell after authenticating to the system, usually by giving your user name and password.

Files read:

- `/etc/profile`
- `~/.bash_profile`, `~/.bash_login` or `~/.profile`: first existing readable file is read
- `~/.bash_logout` upon logout.

Error messages are printed if configuration files exist but are not readable. If a file does not exist, bash searches for the next.

Invoked as an interactive non-login shell

A non-login shell means that you did not have to authenticate to the system. For instance, when you open a terminal using an icon, or a menu item, that is a non-login shell.

Files read:

- `~/.bashrc`

This file is usually referred to in `~/.bash_profile`:

```
if [ -f ~/.bashrc ]; then .  ~/.bashrc; fi
```

See Chapter 7, "Conditional statements" for more information on the **if** construct.

Invoked non-interactively

All scripts use non-interactive shells. They are programmed to do certain tasks and cannot be instructed to do other jobs than those for which they are programmed.

Files read:

- defined by BASH_ENV

PATH is not used to search for this file, so if you want to use it, best refer to it by giving the full path and file name.

Invoked with the sh command

Bash tries to behave as the historical Bourne **sh** program while conforming to the POSIX standard as well.

Files read:

- `/etc/profile`
- `~/.profile`

When invoked interactively, the ENV variable can point to extra startup information.

POSIX mode

This option is enabled either using the **set** built-in:

```
set -o posix
```

or by calling the **bash** program with the `--posix` option. Bash will then try to behave as compliant as possible to the POSIX standard for shells. Setting the POSIXLY_CORRECT variable does the same.

Files read:

- defined by ENV variable.

Invoked remotely

Files read when invoked by **rshd**:

- `~/.bashrc`

 Avoid use of r-tools

Be aware of the dangers when using tools such as **rlogin**, **telnet**, **rsh** and **rcp**. They are intrinsically insecure because confidential data is sent over the network unencrypted. If you need tools for remote execution, file transfer and so on, use an implementation of Secure SHell, generally known as SSH, freely available from <http://www.openssh.org>. Different client programs are available for non-UNIX systems as well; see your local software mirror.

Invoked when UID is not equal to EUID

When the effective user ID (EUID) of the Bash process is different from the user ID of the person invoking the script, Bash does not read any startup files. This situation generally arises with setuid scripts; see the **setuid** man page for more information.

Interactive shells

An interactive shell generally reads from, and writes to, a user's terminal: input and output are connected to a terminal. Bash interactive behavior is started when the **bash** command is called upon without non-option arguments, except when the option is a string to read from or when the shell is invoked to read from standard input, which allows for positional parameters to be set (see Chapter 3, "The Bash environment").

Is this shell interactive?   Test by looking at the content of the special parameter -, it contains an 'i' when the shell is interactive:

```
eddy:~> echo $-
himBH
```

In non-interactive shells, the prompt, PS1, is unset.

Interactive shell behavior   Differences in interactive mode:

- Bash reads startup files.
- Job control enabled by default.
- Prompts are set, PS2 is enabled for multi-line commands, it is usually set to ">". This is also the prompt you get when the shell thinks you entered an unfinished command, for instance when you forget quotes, command structures that cannot be left out, etc.
- Commands are by default read from the command line using **readline**.
- Bash interprets the shell option ignoreeof instead of exiting immediately upon receiving EOF (End Of File).
- Command history and history expansion are enabled by default. History is saved in the file pointed to by HISTFILE when the shell exits. By default, HISTFILE points to ~/.bash_history.
- Alias expansion is enabled.
- In the absence of traps, the SIGTERM signal is ignored.
- In the absence of traps, SIGINT is caught and handled. Thus, typing **Ctrl+C**, for example, will not quit your interactive shell.
- Sending SIGHUP signals to all jobs on exit is configured with the huponexit option.

- Commands are executed upon read.

- Bash checks for mail periodically.

- Bash can be configured to exit when it encounters unreferenced variables. In interactive mode this behavior is disabled.

- When shell built-in commands encounter redirection errors, this will not cause the shell to exit.

- Special built-ins returning errors when used in POSIX mode don't cause the shell to exit. The built-in commands are listed in Section 1.3.

- Failure of **exec** will not exit the shell.

- Parser syntax errors don't cause the shell to exit.

- Simple spell check for the arguments to the **cd** built-in is enabled by default.

- Automatic exit after the length of time specified in the TMOUT variable has passed, is enabled.

More information:

- Section 3.2

- Section 3.6

- See Chapter 12, "Catching signals" for more about signals.

- Section 3.4 discusses the various expansions performed upon entering a command.

Conditionals

Conditional expressions are used by the [[compound command and by the **test** and [built-in commands.

Expressions may be unary or binary. Unary expressions are often used to examine the status of a file. You only need one object, for instance a file, to do the operation on.

There are string operators and numeric comparison operators as well; these are binary operators, requiring two objects to do the operation on. If the FILE argument to one of the primaries is in the form /dev/fd/N, then file descriptor N is checked. If the FILE argument to one of the primaries is one of /dev/stdin, /dev/stdout or /dev/stderr, then file descriptor 0, 1 or 2 respectively is checked.

Conditionals are discussed in detail in Chapter 7, "Conditional statements".

More information about the file descriptors in Section 8.2.2.

Shell arithmetic

The shell allows arithmetic expressions to be evaluated, as one of the shell expansions or by the **let** built-in.

Evaluation is done in fixed-width integers with no check for overflow, though division by 0 is trapped and flagged as an error. The operators and their precedence and associativity are the same as in the C language; see Chapter 3, "The Bash environment".

Aliases

Aliases allow a string to be substituted for a word when it is used as the first word of a simple command. The shell maintains a list of aliases that may be set and unset with the **alias** and **unalias** commands.

Bash always reads at least one complete line of input before executing any of the commands on that line. Aliases are expanded when a command is read, not when it is executed. Therefore, an alias definition appearing on the same line as another command does not take effect until the next line of input is read. The commands following the alias definition on that line are not affected by the new alias.

Aliases are expanded when a function definition is read, not when the function is executed, because a function definition is itself a compound command. As a consequence, aliases defined in a function are not available until after that function is executed.

We will discuss aliases in detail in Section 3.5.

Arrays

Bash provides one-dimensional array variables. Any variable may be used as an array; the **declare** built-in will explicitly declare an array. There is no maximum limit on the size of an array, nor any requirement that members be indexed or assigned contiguously. Arrays are zero-based. See Chapter 10, "More on variables".

Directory stack

The directory stack is a list of recently-visited directories. The **pushd** built-in adds directories to the stack as it changes the current directory, and the **popd** built-in removes specified directories from the stack and changes the current directory to the directory removed.

Content can be displayed issuing the **dirs** command or by checking the content of the DIRSTACK variable.

More information about the workings of this mechanism can be found in the Bash info pages.

The prompt

Bash makes playing with the prompt even more fun. See the section *Controlling the Prompt* in the Bash info pages.

The restricted shell

When invoked as **rbash** or with the `--restricted` or `-r` option, the following happens:

- The **cd** built-in is disabled.
- Setting or unsetting SHELL, PATH, ENV or BASH_ENV is not possible.
- Command names can no longer contain slashes.
- Filenames containing a slash are not allowed with the **.** (**source**) built-in command.
- The **hash** built-in does not accept slashes with the `-p` option.
- Import of functions at startup is disabled.
- SHELLOPTS is ignored at startup.
- Output redirection using $>$, $>|$, $><$, $>$**&**, **&**$>$ and $>>$ is disabled.
- The **exec** built-in is disabled.
- The `-f` and `-d` options are disabled for the **enable** built-in.
- A default PATH cannot be specified with the **command** built-in.
- Turning off restricted mode is not possible.

When a command that is found to be a shell script is executed, **rbash** turns off any restrictions in the shell spawned to execute the script.

More information:

- Section 3.2
- Section 3.6
- **Info Bash → Basic Shell Features → Redirections**
- Section 8.2.2: advanced redirection

1.3 Executing commands

Bash determines the type of program that is to be executed. Normal programs are system commands that exist in compiled form on your system. When such a program is executed, a new process is created because Bash makes an exact copy of itself. This child process has the same environment as its parent, only the process ID number is different. This procedure is called *forking*.

After the forking process, the address space of the child process is overwritten with the new process data. This is done through an *exec* call to the system.

The *fork-and-exec* mechanism thus switches an old command with a new, while the environment in which the new program is executed remains the same, including configuration of input and output devices, environment variables and priority. This mechanism is used to create all UNIX processes, so it also applies to the Linux operating system. Even the first process, **init**, with process ID 1, is forked during the boot procedure in the so-called *bootstrapping* procedure.

1.3.1 Shell built-in commands

Built-in commands are contained within the shell itself. When the name of a built-in command is used as the first word of a simple command, the shell executes the command directly, without creating a new process. Built-in commands are necessary to implement functionality impossible or inconvenient to obtain with separate utilities.

Bash supports 3 types of built-in commands:

- Bourne Shell built-ins:

  :, ., break, cd, continue, eval, exec, exit, export, getopts, hash, pwd, readonly, return, set, shift, test, [, times, trap, umask and **unset**.

- Bash built-in commands:

  alias, bind, builtin, command, declare, echo, enable, help, let, local, logout, printf, read, shopt, type, typeset, ulimit and **unalias**.

- Special built-in commands:

  When Bash is executing in POSIX mode, the special built-ins differ from other built-in commands in three respects:

  1. Special built-ins are found before shell functions during command lookup.
  2. If a special built-in returns an error status, a non-interactive shell exits.
  3. Assignment statements preceding the command stay in effect in the shell environment after the command completes.

  The POSIX special built-ins are **:, ., break, continue, eval, exec, exit, export, readonly, return, set, shift, trap** and **unset**.

Most of these built-ins will be discussed in the next chapters. For those commands for which this is not the case, we refer to the Info pages.

1.3.2 Executing programs from a script

When the program being executed is a shell script, bash will create a new bash process using a *fork*. This subshell reads the lines from the shell script one line at a time. Commands on each line are read, interpreted and executed as if they would have come directly from the keyboard.

While the subshell processes each line of the script, the parent shell waits for its child process to finish. When there are no more lines in the shell script to read, the subshell terminates. The parent shell awakes and displays a new prompt.

1.4 Shell building blocks

If input is not commented, the shell reads it and divides it into words and operators, employing quoting rules to define the meaning of each character of input. Then these words and operators are translated into commands and other constructs, which return an exit status available for inspection or processing. The above fork-and-exec scheme is only applied after the shell has analyzed input in the following way:

- The shell reads its input from a file, from a string or from the user's terminal.

- Input is broken up into words and operators, obeying the quoting rules; see Chapter 3, "The Bash environment". These tokens are separated by *metacharacters*. Alias expansion is performed.

- The shell *parses* (analyzes and substitutes) the tokens into simple and compound commands.

- Bash performs various shell expansions, breaking the expanded tokens into lists of filenames and commands and arguments.

- Redirection is performed if necessary, redirection operators and their operands are removed from the argument list.

- Commands are executed.

- Optionally the shell waits for the command to complete and collects its exit status.

Shell commands

A simple shell command such as **touch file1 file2 file3** consists of the command itself followed by arguments, separated by spaces.

More complex shell commands are composed of simple commands arranged together in a variety of ways: in a pipeline in which the output of one command becomes the input of a second, in a loop or conditional construct, or in some other grouping. A couple of examples:

```
ls | more

gunzip file.tar.gz | tar xvf -
```

Shell functions

Shell functions are a way to group commands for later execution using a single name for the group. They are executed just like a "regular" command. When the name of a shell function is used as a simple command name, the list of commands associated with that function name is executed.

Shell functions are executed in the current shell context; no new process is created to interpret them.

Functions are explained in Chapter 11, "Functions".

Shell parameters

A parameter is an entity that stores values. It can be a name, a number or a special value. For the shell's purpose, a variable is a parameter that stores a name. A variable has a value and zero or more attributes. Variables are created with the **declare** shell built-in command.

If no value is given, a variable is assigned the null string. Variables can only be removed with the **unset** built-in.

Assigning variables is discussed in Section 3.2, advanced use of variables in Chapter 10, "More on variables".

Shell expansions

Shell expansion is performed after each command line has been split into tokens. These are the expansions performed:

- Brace expansion
- Tilde expansion
- Parameter and variable expansion
- Command substitution
- Arithmetic expansion
- Word splitting
- Filename expansion

We'll discuss these expansion types in detail in Section 3.4.

Redirections

Before a command is executed, its input and output may be redirected using a special notation interpreted by the shell. Redirection may also be used to open and close files for the current shell execution environment.

Executing commands

When executing a command, the words that the parser has marked as variable assignments (preceding the command name) and redirections are saved for later reference. Words that are not variable assignments or redirections are expanded; the first remaining word after expansion is taken to be the name of the command and the rest are arguments to that command. Then redirections are performed, then strings assigned to variables are expanded. If no command name results, variables will affect the current shell environment.

An important part of the tasks of the shell is to search for commands. Bash does this as follows:

- Check whether the command contains slashes. If not, first check with the function list to see if it contains a command by the name we are looking for.

- If command is not a function, check for it in the built-in list.

- If command is neither a function nor a built-in, look for it analyzing the directories listed in PATH. Bash uses a *hash table* (data storage area in memory) to remember the full path names of executables so extensive PATH searches can be avoided.

- If the search is unsuccessful, bash prints an error message and returns an exit status of 127.

- If the search was successful or if the command contains slashes, the shell executes the command in a separate execution environment.

- If execution fails because the file is not executable and not a directory, it is assumed to be a shell script.

- If the command was not begun asynchronously, the shell waits for the command to complete and collects its exit status.

Shell scripts

When a file containing shell commands is used as the first non-option argument when invoking Bash (without -c or -s, this will create a non-interactive shell. This shell first searches for the script file in the current directory, then looks in PATH if the file cannot be found there.

1.5 Developing good scripts

This guide is mainly about the last shell building block, scripts. Some general considerations before we continue:

1. A script should run without errors.

2. It should perform the task for which it is intended.

3. Program logic is clearly defined and apparent.

4. A script does not do unnecessary work.

5. Scripts should be reusable.

1.5.1 Structure

The structure of a shell script is very flexible. Even though in Bash a lot of freedom is granted, you must ensure correct logic, flow control and efficiency so that users executing the script can do so easily and correctly.

When starting on a new script, ask yourself the following questions:

- Will I be needing any information from the user or from the user's environment?

- How will I store that information?

- Are there any files that need to be created? Where and with which permissions and ownerships?

- What commands will I use? When using the script on different systems, do all these systems have these commands in the required versions?

- Does the user need any notifications? When and why?

1.5.2 Terminology

The table below gives an overview of programming terms that you need to be familiar with:

Table 1.1: Overview of programming terms

Term	What is it?
Command control	Testing exit status of a command in order to determine whether a portion of the program should be executed.
Conditional branch	Logical point in the program when a condition determines what happens next.
Logic flow	The overall design of the program. Determines logical sequence of tasks so that the result is successful and controlled.

| Loop | Part of the program that is performed zero or more times. |
| User input | Information provided by an external source while the program is running, can be stored and recalled when needed. |

1.5.3 A word on order and logic

In order to speed up the developing process, the logical order of a program should be thought over in advance. This is your first step when developing a script.

A number of methods can be used; one of the most common is working with lists. Itemizing the list of tasks involved in a program allows you to describe each process. Individual tasks can be referenced by their item number.

Using your own spoken language to pin down the tasks to be executed by your program will help you to create an understandable form of your program. Later, you can replace the everyday language statements with shell language words and constructs.

The example below shows such a logic flow design. It describes the rotation of log files. This example shows a possible repetitive loop, controlled by the number of base log files you want to rotate:

1. Do you want to rotate logs?

    (a) If yes:

        i. Enter directory name containing the logs to be rotated.

        ii. Enter base name of the log file.

        iii. Enter number of days logs should be kept.

        iv. Make settings permanent in user's crontab file.

    (b) If no, go to step 3.

2. Do you want to rotate another set of logs?

    (a) If yes: repeat step 1.

    (b) If no: go to step 3.

3. Exit

The user should provide information for the program to do something. Input from the user must be obtained and stored. The user should be notified that his crontab will change.

1.5.4   An example Bash script: mysystem.sh

The `mysystem.sh` script below executes some well-known commands (**date, w, uname, uptime**) to display information about you and your machine.

```
tom:~> cat -n mysystem.sh
     1  #!/bin/bash
     2  clear
     3  echo "This is information provided by mysystem.sh.  Program starts now."
     4
     5  echo "Hello, $USER"
     6  echo
     7
     8  echo "Today's date is `date`, this is week `date +"%V"`."
     9  echo
    10
    11  echo "These users are currently connected:"
    12  w | cut -d " " -f 1 - | grep -v USER | sort -u
    13  echo
    14
    15  echo "This is `uname -s` running on a `uname -m` processor."
    16  echo
    17
    18  echo "This is the uptime information:"
    19  uptime
    20  echo
    21
    22  echo "That's all folks!"
```

A script always starts with the same two characters, "#!". After that, the shell that will execute the commands following the first line is defined. This script starts with clearing the screen on line 2. Line 3 makes it print a message, informing the user about what is going to happen. Line 5 greets the user. Lines 6, 9, 13, 16 and 20 are only there for orderly output display purposes. Line 8 prints the current date and the number of the week. Line 11 is again an informative message, like lines 3, 18 and 22. Line 12 formats the output of the **w**; line 15 shows operating system and CPU information. Line 19 gives the uptime and load information.

Both **echo** and **printf** are Bash built-in commands. The first always exits with a 0 status, and simply prints arguments followed by an end of line character on the standard output, while the latter allows for definition of a formatting string and gives a non-zero exit status code upon failure.

This is the same script using the **printf** built-in:

```
tom:~> cat mysystem.sh
#!/bin/bash
clear
printf "This is information provided by mysystem.sh.  Program starts now."

printf "Hello, $USER.\n\n"

printf "Today's date is `date`, this is week `date +"%V"`.\n\n"

printf "These users are currently connected:\n"
w | cut -d " " -f 1 - | grep -v USER | sort -u
printf "\n"

printf "This is `uname -s` running on a `uname -m` processor.\n\n"

printf "This is the uptime information:\n"
uptime
printf "\n"

printf "That's all folks!\n"
```

Creating user friendly scripts by means of inserting messages is treated in Chapter 8, "Writing interactive scripts".

Standard location of the Bourne Again shell

This implies that the **bash** program is installed in /bin.

If stdout is not available

If you execute a script from cron, supply full path names and redirect output and errors. Since the shell runs in non-interactive mode, any errors will cause the script to exit prematurely if you don't think about this.

The following chapters will discuss the details of the above scripts.

1.5.5   Example init script

An init script starts system services on UNIX and Linux machines. The system log daemon, the power management daemon, the name and mail daemons are common examples. These scripts, also known as startup scripts, are stored in a specific location on your system, such as /etc/rc.d/init.d or /etc/init.d. Init, the initial process, reads its configuration files and decides which services to start or stop in each run level. A run level is a configuration of processes; each system has a single user run level, for instance, for performing administrative tasks, for which the system has to be in an unused state as much as possible, such as recovering a critical file system from a backup. Reboot and shutdown run levels are usually also configured.

The tasks to be executed upon starting a service or stopping it are listed in the startup scripts. It is one of the system administrator's tasks to configure **init**, so that services are started and stopped at the correct moment. When confronted with this task, you need a good understanding of the startup and shutdown procedures on your system. We therefore advise that you read the man pages for **init** and `inittab` before starting on your own initialization scripts.

Here is a very simple example, that will play a sound upon starting and stopping your machine:

```
#!/bin/bash

# This script is for /etc/rc.d/init.d
# Link in rc3.d/S99audio-greeting and rc0.d/K01audio-greeting

case "$1" in
'start')
  cat /usr/share/audio/at_your_service.au > /dev/audio
  ;;
'stop')
  cat /usr/share/audio/oh_no_not_again.au > /dev/audio
  ;;
esac
exit 0
```

The **case** statement often used in this kind of script is described in Section 7.6.

1.6 Summary

Bash is the GNU shell, compatible with the Bourne shell and incorporating many useful features from other shells. When the shell is started, it reads its configuration files. The most important are:

- `/etc/profile`
- `~/.bash_profile`
- `~/.bashrc`

Bash behaves different when in interactive mode and also has a POSIX compliant and a restricted mode.

Shell commands can be split up in three groups: the shell functions, shell built-ins and existing commands in a directory on your system. Bash supports additional built-ins not found in the plain Bourne shell.

Shell scripts consist of these commands arranged as shell syntax dictates. Scripts are read and executed line per line and should have a logical structure.

1.7 Exercises

These are some exercises to warm you up for the next chapter:

1. Where is the **bash** program located on your system?

2. Use the `--version` option to find out which version you are running.

3. Which shell configuration files are read when you login to your system using the graphical user interface and then opening a terminal window?

4. Are the following shells interactive shells? Are they login shells?

   - A shell opened by clicking on the background of your graphical desktop, selecting "Terminal" or such from a menu.

   - A shell that you get after issuing the command **ssh** `localhost`.

   - A shell that you get when logging in to the console in text mode.

   - A shell obtained by the command **xterm &**.

   - A shell opened by the **mysystem.sh** script.

   - A shell that you get on a remote host, for which you didn't have to give the login and/or password because you use SSH and maybe SSH keys.

5. Can you explain why **bash** does not exit when you type **Ctrl+C** on the command line?

6. Display directory stack content.

7. If it is not yet the case, set your prompt so that it displays your location in the file system hierarchy, for instance add this line to `~/.bashrc`:

   ```
   export PS1="\u@\h \w>"
   ```

8. Display hashed commands for your current shell session.

9. How many processes are currently running on your system? Use **ps** and **wc**, the first line of output of **ps** is not a process!

10. How to display the system hostname? Only the name, nothing more!

Chapter 2

Writing and debugging scripts

After going through this chapter, you will be able to:

- *Write a simple script*
- *Define the shell type that should execute the script*
- *Put comments in a script*
- *Change permissions on a script*
- *Execute and debug a script*

2.1 Creating and running a script

A shell script is a sequence of commands for which you have a repeated use. This sequence is typically executed by entering the name of the script on the command line. Alternatively, you can use scripts to automate tasks using the cron facility. Another use for scripts is in the UNIX boot and shutdown procedure, where operation of daemons and services are defined in init scripts.

To create a shell script, open a new empty file in your editor. Any text editor will do: **vim**, **emacs**, **gedit**, **dtpad** et cetera are all valid. You might want to chose a more advanced editor like **vim** or **emacs**, however, because these can be configured to recognize shell and Bash syntax and can be a great help in preventing those errors that beginners frequently make, such as forgetting brackets and semicolons.

Put UNIX commands in the new empty file, like you would enter them on the command line. As discussed in the previous chapter (see Section 1.3), commands can be shell functions, shell built-ins, UNIX commands and other scripts.

Give your script a sensible name that gives a hint about what the script does. Make sure that your script name does not conflict with existing commands. In order to ensure that no confusion can rise, script names often end in .sh; even so, there might be other scripts on your system with the same name as the one you chose. Check using **which**, **whereis** and other commands for finding information about programs and files:

```
which -a script_name

whereis script_name

locate script_name
```

2.1.1   script1.sh

In this example we use the **echo** Bash built-in to inform the user about what is going to happen, before the task that will create the output is executed. It is strongly advised to inform users about what a script is doing, in order to prevent them from becoming nervous *because the script is not doing anything*. We will return to the subject of notifying users in Chapter 8, "Writing interactive scripts".

Write this script for yourself as well. It might be a good idea to create a directory ˜/scripts to hold your scripts. Add the directory to the contents of the PATH variable:

```
export PATH="$PATH:~/scripts"
```

If you are just getting started with Bash, use a text editor that uses different colours for different shell constructs. Syntax highlighting is supported by **vim**,

```
#!/bin/bash

clear

echo "The script starts now."

echo "Hi, $USER!"
echo

echo "I will now fetch you a list of connected users:"
echo
w
echo

echo "I'm setting two variables now."
COLOUR="black"
VALUE="9"
echo "This is a string: $COLOUR"
echo "And this is a number: $VALUE"
echo

echo "I'm giving you back your prompt now."
echo
~
~
~
                                        8,4-20          All
```

Figure 2.1: script1.sh

gvim, (x)emacs, kwrite and many other editors; check the documentation of your favorite editor.

 Different prompts

> The prompts throughout this course vary depending on the author's mood. This resembles much more real life situations than the standard educational $ prompt. The only convention we stick to, is that the *root* prompt ends in a hash mark (#).

2.1.2 Executing the script

The script should have execute permissions for the correct owners in order to be runnable. When setting permissions, check that you really obtained the permissions that you want. When this is done, the script can run like any other command:

```
willy:~/scripts> chmod u+x script1.sh

willy:~/scripts> ls -l script1.sh
-rwxrw-r--     1 willy    willy         456 Dec 24 17:11 script1.sh

willy:~> script1.sh
The script starts now.
Hi, willy!

I will now fetch you a list of connected users:

  3:38pm  up 18 days,  5:37,  4 users,  load average: 0.12, 0.22, 0.15
USER       TTY       FROM      LOGIN@    IDLE   JCPU    PCPU   WHAT
root       tty2      -         Sat 2pm   4:25m  0.24s   0.05s  -bash
willy      :0        -         Sat 2pm   ?      0.00s   ?      -
willy      pts/3     -         Sat 2pm   3:33m 36.39s  36.39s  BitchX willy ir
willy      pts/2     -         Sat 2pm   3:33m  0.13s   0.06s  /usr/bin/screen

I'm setting two variables now.
This is a string: black
And this is a number: 9

I'm giving you back your prompt now.

willy:~/scripts> echo $COLOUR

willy:~/scripts> echo $VALUE

willy:~/scripts>
```

This is the most common way to execute a script. It is preferred to execute the script like this in a subshell. The variables, functions and aliases created in this subshell are only known to the particular bash session of that subshell. When that shell exits and the parent regains control, everything is cleaned up and all changes to the state of the shell made by the script, are forgotten.

If you did not put the scripts directory in your PATH, and . (the current directory) is not in the PATH either, you can activate the script like this:

./script_name.sh

A script can also explicitly be executed by a given shell, but generally we only do this if we want to obtain special behavior, such as checking if the script works with another shell or printing traces for debugging:

rbash script_name.sh

sh script_name.sh

bash -x script_name.sh

The specified shell will start as a subshell of your current shell and execute the script. This is done when you want the script to start up with specific options or under specific conditions which are not specified in the script.

If you don't want to start a new shell but execute the script in the current shell, you *source* it:

```
source script_name.sh
```

 source = .

The Bash **source** built-in is a synonym for the Bourne shell **.** (dot) command.

The script does not need execute permission in this case. Commands are executed in the current shell context, so any changes made to your environment will be visible when the script finishes execution:

```
willy:~/scripts> source script1.sh
--output ommitted--

willy:~/scripts> echo $VALUE
9

willy:~/scripts>
```

2.2 Script basics

 Which shell will run the script?

When running a script in a subshell, you should define which shell should run the script. The shell type in which you wrote the script might not be the default on your system, so commands you entered might result in errors when executed by the wrong shell.

The first line of the script determines the shell to start. The first two characters of the first line should be #!, then follows the path to the shell that should interpret the commands that follow. Blank lines are also considered to be lines, so don't start your script with an empty line.

For the purpose of this course, all scripts will start with the line

```
#!/bin/bash
```

As noted before, this implies that the Bash executable can be found in /bin.

2.2.1 Adding comments

You should be aware of the fact that you might not be the only person reading your code. A lot of users and system administrators run scripts that were written by other people. If they want to see how you did it, comments are useful to enlighten the reader.

Comments also make your own life easier. Say that you had to read a lot of man pages in order to achieve a particular result with some command that you used in your script. You won't remember how it worked if you need to change your script after a few weeks or months, unless you have commented what you did, how you did it and/or why you did it.

Take the `script1.sh` example and copy it to `commented-script1.sh`, which we edit so that the comments reflect what the script does. Everything the shell encounters after a hash mark on a line is ignored and only visible upon opening the shell script file:

```
#!/bin/bash
# This script clears the terminal, displays a greeting and gives
# information about currently connected users.  The two example
# variables are set and displayed.

clear                   # clear terminal window

echo "The script starts now."

echo "Hi, $USER!"    # dollar sign is used to get content of variable
echo

echo "I will now fetch you a list of connected users:"
echo
w                       # show who is logged on and
echo                    # what they are doing
echo "I'm setting two variables now."
COLOUR="black"                          # set a local shell variable
VALUE="9"                               # set a local shell variable
echo "This is a string: $COLOUR"        # display content of variable
echo "And this is a number: $VALUE"     # display content of variable
echo

echo "I'm giving you back your prompt now."
echo
```

In a decent script, the first lines are usually comment about what to expect. Then each big chunk of commands will be commented as needed for clarity's sake. Linux init scripts, as an example, in your system's `init.d` directory, are usually well commented since they have to be readable and editable by everyone running Linux.

2.3 Debugging Bash scripts

When things don't go according to plan, you need to determine what exactly causes the script to fail. Bash provides extensive debugging features. The most common is to start up the subshell with the -x option, which will run the entire script in debug mode. Traces of each command plus its arguments are printed to standard output after the commands have been expanded but before they are executed.

This is the `commented-script1.sh` script ran in debug mode. Note again that the added comments are not visible in the output of the script.

```
willy:~/scripts> bash -x script1.sh
+ clear

+ echo 'The script starts now.'
The script starts now.
+ echo 'Hi, willy!'
Hi, willy!
+ echo

+ echo 'I will now fetch you a list of connected users:'
I will now fetch you a list of connected users:
+ echo

+ w
  4:50pm  up 18 days,  6:49,  4 users,  load average: 0.58, 0.62, 0.40
USER      TTY      FROM     LOGIN@   IDLE    JCPU    PCPU  WHAT
root      tty2     -        Sat 2pm  5:36m   0.24s   0.05s -bash
willy     :0       -        Sat 2pm  ?       0.00s   ?     -
willy     pts/3    -        Sat 2pm  43:13   36.82s  36.82s BitchX willy ir
willy     pts/2    -        Sat 2pm  43:13   0.13s   0.06s /usr/bin/screen
+ echo

+ echo 'I'\''m setting two variables now.'
I'm setting two variables now.
+ COLOUR=black
+ VALUE=9
+ echo 'This is a string: '
This is a string:
+ echo 'And this is a number: '
And this is a number:
+ echo

+ echo 'I'\''m giving you back your prompt now.'
I'm giving you back your prompt now.
+ echo
```

2.3.1 Debugging on part(s) of the script

Using the **set** Bash built-in you can run in normal mode those portions of the script of which you are sure they are without fault, and display debugging information only for troublesome zones. Say we are not sure what the **w** command will do in the example `commented-script1.sh`, then we could enclose it in the script like this:

```
set -x          # activate debugging from here
w
set +x          # stop debugging from here
```

Output then looks like this:

```
willy: ~/scripts> script1.sh
The script starts now.
Hi, willy!

I will now fetch you a list of connected users:

+ w
  5:00pm  up 18 days,  7:00,  4 users,  load average: 0.79, 0.39, 0.33
USER      TTY       FROM      LOGIN@    IDLE    JCPU    PCPU  WHAT
root      tty2      -         Sat 2pm   5:47m   0.24s   0.05s -bash
willy     :0        -         Sat 2pm   ?       0.00s   ?     -
willy     pts/3     -         Sat 2pm   54:02   36.88s  36.88s BitchX willyke
willy     pts/2     -         Sat 2pm   54:02   0.13s   0.06s /usr/bin/screen
+ set +x

I'm setting two variables now.
This is a string:
And this is a number:

I'm giving you back your prompt now.

willy: ~/scripts>
```

You can switch debugging mode on and off as many times as you want within the same script.

The table below gives an overview of other useful Bash options:

Table 2.1: Overview of set debugging options

Short notation	Long notation	Result
set -f	set -o noglob	Disable file name generation using metacharacters (globbing).
set -v	set -o verbose	Prints shell input lines as they are read.
set -x	set -o xtrace	Print command traces before executing command.

The dash is used to activate a shell option and a plus to deactivate it. Don't let this confuse you!

In the example below, we demonstrate these options on the command line:

```
willy:~/scripts> set -v

willy:~/scripts> ls
ls
commented-scripts.sh     script1.sh

willy:~/scripts> set +v
set +v

willy:~/scripts> ls *
commented-scripts.sh     script1.sh

willy:~/scripts> set -f

willy:~/scripts> ls *
ls: *: No such file or directory

willy:~/scripts> touch *

willy:~/scripts> ls
*    commented-scripts.sh     script1.sh

willy:~/scripts> rm *

willy:~/scripts> ls
commented-scripts.sh     script1.sh
```

Alternatively, these modes can be specified in the script itself, by adding the desired options to the first line shell declaration. Options can be combined, as is usually the case with UNIX commands:

```
#!/bin/bash -xv
```

Once you found the buggy part of your script, you can add **echo** statements before each command of which you are unsure, so that you will see exactly where and why things don't work. In the example `commented-script1.sh` script, it could be done like this, still assuming that the displaying of users gives us problems:

```
echo "debug message: now attempting to start w command"; w
```

In more advanced scripts, the **echo** can be inserted to display the content of variables at different stages in the script, so that flaws can be detected:

```
echo "Variable VARNAME is now set to $VARNAME."
```

2.4 Summary

A shell script is a reusable series of commands put in an executable text file. Any text editor can be used to write scripts.

Scripts start with #! followed by the path to the shell executing the commands from the script. Comments are added to a script for your own future reference, and also to make it understandable for other users. It is better to have too many explanations than not enough.

Debugging a script can be done using shell options. Shell options can be used for partial debugging or for analyzing the entire script. Inserting **echo** commands at strategic locations is also a common troubleshooting technique.

2.5 Exercises

This exercise will help you to create your first script.

1. Write a script using your favorite editor. The script should display the path to your homedirectory and the terminal type that you are using. Additionally it shows all the services started up in runlevel 3 on your system. (hint: use HOME, TERM and **ls /etc/rc3.d/S***)

2. Add comments in your script.

3. Add information for the users of your script.

4. Change permissions on your script so that you can run it.

5. Run the script in normal mode and in debug mode. It should run without errors.

6. Make errors in your script: see what happens if you misspell commands, if you leave out the first line or put something unintelligible there, or if you misspell shell variable names or write them in lower case characters after they have been declared in capitals. Check what the debug comments say about this.

Chapter 3

The Bash environment

In this chapter we will discuss the various ways in which the Bash environment can be influenced:

- *Editing shell initialization files*
- *Using variables*
- *Using different quote styles*
- *Perform arithmetic calculations*
- *Assigning aliases*
- *Using expansion and substitution*

3.1 Shell initialization files

Depending on how it is invoked, Bash executes several configuration files before it begins a script or interactive session.

/etc/profile

When invoked interactively with the --login option or when invoked as **sh**, Bash reads the /etc/profile instructions. These usually set the shell variables PATH, USER, MAIL, HOSTNAME and HISTSIZE.

On some systems, the **umask** value is configured in /etc/profile; on other systems this file holds pointers to other configuration files such as:

- /etc/inputrc, the system-wide Readline initialization file where you can configure the command line bell-style.

- the /etc/profile.d directory, which contains files configuring system-wide behavior of specific programs.

All settings that you want to apply to all your users' environments should be in this file. It might look like this:

```
# /etc/profile

# System wide environment and startup programs, for login setup

PATH=$PATH:/usr/X11R6/bin

# No core files by default
ulimit -S -c 0 > /dev/null 2>&1

USER="`id -un`"
LOGNAME=$USER
MAIL="/var/spool/mail/$USER"

HOSTNAME=`/bin/hostname`
HISTSIZE=1000

# Keyboard, bell, display style: the readline config file:
if [ -z "$INPUTRC" -a ! -f "$HOME/.inputrc" ]; then
    INPUTRC=/etc/inputrc
fi

PS1="\u@\h \W"

export PATH USER LOGNAME MAIL HOSTNAME HISTSIZE INPUTRC PS1

# Source initialization files for specific programs (ls, vim, less, ...)
for i in /etc/profile.d/*.sh ; do
    if [ -r "$i" ]; then
        . $i
    fi
done

# Settings for program initialization
source /etc/java.conf
export NPX_PLUGIN_PATH="$JRE_HOME/plugin/ns4plugin/:/usr/lib/netscape/plugins"
```

```
PAGER="/usr/bin/less"

unset i
```

This configuration file sets some basic shell environment variables as well as some variables required by users running Java and/or Java applications in their web browser. See Section 3.2.

See Chapter 7, "Conditional statements" for more on the conditional **if** used in this file; Chapter 9, "Repetitive tasks" discusses loops such as the **for** construct.

The Bash source contains sample profile files for general or individual use. These and the one in the example above need changes in order for them to work in your environment!

/etc/bashrc

On systems offering multiple types of shells, it might be better to put Bash-specific configurations in this file, since /etc/profile is also read by other shells, such as the Bourne shell. Errors generated by shells that don't understand the Bash syntax are prevented by splitting the configuration files for the different types of shells. In such cases, the user's ~/.bashrc might point to /etc/bashrc in order to include it in the shell initialization process upon login.

You might also find that /etc/profile on your system only holds shell environment and program startup settings, while /etc/bashrc contains system-wide definitions for shell functions and aliases. The /etc/bashrc file might be referred to in /etc/profile or in individual user shell initialization files.

The source contains sample bashrc files, or you might find a copy in /usr/share/doc/bash-2.05b/startup-files. This is part of the bashrc that comes with the Bash documentation:

```
alias ll='ls -l'
alias dir='ls -ba'
alias c='clear'
alias ls='ls --color'
alias mroe='more'
alias pdw='pwd'
alias sl='ls --color'
```

```
pskill()
{
        local pid

        pid=$(ps -ax | grep $1 | grep -v grep | gawk '{ print $1 }')
        echo -n "killing $1 (process $pid)..."
        kill -9 $pid
        echo "slaughtered."
}
```

Apart from general aliases, it contains useful aliases which make commands work even if you misspell them. We will discuss aliases in Section 3.5.2. This file contains a function, **pskill**; functions will be studied in detail in Chapter 11, "Functions".

3.1.1   Individual user configuration files

In addition to the system-wide configuration files, Bash reads several optional configuration files in the current user's home directory.

 I don't have these files?!

These files might not be in your home directory by default; create them if needed.

˜/.bash_profile

This is the preferred configuration file for configuring user environments individually. In this file, users can add extra configuration options or change default settings:

```
franky~> cat .bash_profile
##################################################################
#                                                                #
#    .bash_profile file                                          #
#                                                                #
#    Executed from the bash shell when you log in.               #
#                                                                #
##################################################################
```

```
source ~/.bashrc
source ~/.bash_login
case "$OS" in
  IRIX)
    stty sane dec
    stty erase
    ;;
#  SunOS)
#    stty erase
#    ;;
  *)
    stty sane
    ;;
esac
```

This user configures the backspace character for login on different operating systems. Apart from that, the user's .bashrc and .bash_login are read.

~/.bash_login

This file contains specific settings that are normally only executed when you log in to the system. In the example, we use it to configure the **umask** value and to show a list of connected users upon login. This user also gets the calendar for the current month:

```
##########################################################################
#                                                                        #
#    Bash_login file                                                     #
#                                                                        #
#    commands to perform from the bash shell at login time               #
#    (sourced from .bash_profile)                                        #
#                                                                        #
##########################################################################
#    file protection
umask 002        # all to me, read to group and others
#    miscellaneous
w
cal `date +"%m"` `date +"%Y"`
```

In the absence of ~/.bash_profile, this file will be read.

~/.profile

In the absence of ~/.bash_profile and ~/.bash_login, ~/.profile is read. It can hold the same configurations, which are then also accessible by other shells. Mind that other shells might not understand the Bash syntax.

~/.bashrc

Today, it is more common to use a non-login shell, for instance when logged in graphically using X terminal windows. Upon opening such a window, the user does not have to provide a user name or password; no authentication is done. Bash searches for ~/.bashrc when this happens, so it is referred to in the files read upon login as well, which means you don't have to enter the same settings in multiple files.

In this user's .bashrc a couple of aliases are defined and variables for specific programs are set after the system-wide /etc/bashrc is read:

```
franky ~> cat .bashrc
# /home/franky/.bashrc

# Source global definitions
if [ -f /etc/bashrc ]; then
        . /etc/bashrc

fi
# shell options

set -o noclobber
# my shell variables

export PS1="\[\033[1;44m\]\u \w\[\033[0m\] "
export PATH="$PATH:~/bin:~/scripts"

# my aliases

alias cdrecord='cdrecord -dev 0,0,0 -speed=8'
alias ss='ssh octarine'
alias ll='ls -la'
# mozilla fix

MOZILLA_FIVE_HOME=/usr/lib/mozilla
LD_LIBRARY_PATH=/usr/lib/mozilla:/usr/lib/mozilla/plugins
MOZ_DIST_BIN=/usr/lib/mozilla
MOZ_PROGRAM=/usr/lib/mozilla/mozilla-bin
export MOZILLA_FIVE_HOME LD_LIBRARY_PATH MOZ_DIST_BIN MOZ_PROGRAM

# font fix
alias xt='xterm -bg black -fg white &'

# BitchX settings
export IRCNAME="frnk"

# THE END
franky ~>
```

More examples can be found in the Bash package. Remember that sample files might need changes in order to work in your environment.

Aliases are discussed in Section 3.5.

~/.bash_logout

This file contains specific instructions for the logout procedure. In the example, the terminal window is cleared upon logout. This is useful for remote connections, which will leave a clean window after closing them.

```
franky ~> cat .bash_logout
#######################################################################
#                                                                     #
#    Bash_logout file                                                 #
#                                                                     #
#    commands to perform from the bash shell at logout time           #
#                                                                     #
#######################################################################
clear
franky ~>
```

3.1.2   Changing shell configuration files

When making changes to any of the above files, users have to either reconnect to the system or **source** the altered file for the changes to take effect. By interpreting the script this way, changes are applied to the current shell session:

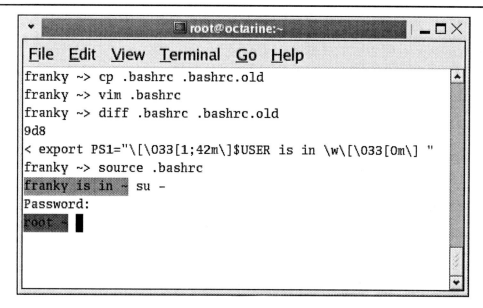

Figure 3.1: Different prompts for different users

Most shell scripts execute in a private environment: variables are not inherited by child processes unless they are exported by the parent shell. Sourcing a file containing shell commands is a way of applying changes to your own environment and setting variables in the current shell.

This example also demonstrates the use of different prompt settings by different users. In this case, red means danger. When you have a green prompt, don't worry too much.

Note that **source resourcefile** is the same as **. resourcefile**.

Should you get lost in all these configuration files, and find yourself confronted with settings of which the origin is not clear, use **echo** statements, just like for debugging scripts; see Section 2.3.1. You might add lines like this:

```
echo "Now executing .bash_profile.."
```

or like this:

```
echo "Now setting PS1 in .bashrc:"
export PS1="[some value]"
echo "PS1 is now set to $PS1"
```

3.2 Variables

As seen in the examples above, shell variables are in uppercase characters by convention. Bash keeps a list of two types of variables:

Global variables

Global variables or environment variables are available in all shells. The **env** or **printenv** commands can be used to display environment variables. These programs come with the *sh-utils* package.

Below is a typical output:

```
franky ~> printenv
CC=gcc
CDPATH=.:~:/usr/local:/usr:/
CFLAGS=-O2 -fomit-frame-pointer
COLORTERM=gnome-terminal
CXXFLAGS=-O2 -fomit-frame-pointer
DISPLAY=:0
DOMAIN=hq.soti.org
```

```
e=
TOR=vi
FCEDIT=vi
FIGNORE=.o:~
G_BROKEN_FILENAMES=1
GDK_USE_XFT=1
GDMSESSION=Default
GNOME_DESKTOP_SESSION_ID=Default

[continues]
```

Local variables

Local variables are only available in the current shell. Using the **set** built-in command without any options will display a list of all variables (including environment variables) and functions. The output will be sorted according to the current locale and displayed in a reusable format.

Below is a diff file made by comparing **printenv** and **set** output, after leaving out the functions which are also displayed by the **set** command:

```
franky ~>  diff set.sorted printenv.sorted | grep "<" | awk '{ print $2 } '
BASE=/nethome/franky/.Shell/hq.soti.org/octarine.aliases
BASH=/bin/bash
BASH_VERSINFO=([0]="2"
BASH_VERSION='2.05b.0(1)-release'
COLUMNS=80
DIRSTACK=()
DO_FORTUNE=
EUID=504
GROUPS=()
HERE=/home/franky
HISTFILE=/nethome/franky/.bash_history
HOSTTYPE=i686
IFS=$'
LINES=24
MACHTYPE=i686-pc-linux-gnu
OPTERR=1
OPTIND=1
OSTYPE=linux-gnu
PIPESTATUS=([0]="0")
PPID=10099
PS4='+
PWD_REAL='pwd
SHELLOPTS=braceexpand:emacs:hashall:histexpand:history:interactive-comments:monitor
THERE=/home/franky
UID=504
```

 Awk

the GNU Awk programming language is explained in Chapter 6, "The GNU awk programming language".

Variables by content

Apart from dividing variables in local and global variables, we can also divide them in categories according to the sort of content the variable contains. In this respect, variables come in 4 types:

- String variables
- Integer variables
- Constant variables
- Array variables

We'll discuss these types in Chapter 10, "More on variables". For now, we will work with integer and string values for our variables.

3.2.1 Creating variables

Variables are case sensitive and capitalized by default. Giving local variables a lowercase name is a convention which is sometimes applied. However, you are free to use the names you want or to mix cases. Variables can also contain digits, but a name starting with a digit is not allowed:

```
prompt> export 1number=1
bash: export: '1number=1': not a valid identifier
```

To set a variable in the shell, use

```
VARNAME="value"
```

Putting spaces around the equal sign will cause errors. It is a good habit to quote content strings when assigning values to variables: this will reduce the chance that you make errors.

Some examples using upper and lower cases, numbers and spaces:

```
franky ~> MYVAR1="2"

franky ~> echo $MYVAR1
2

franky ~> first_name="Franky"

franky ~> echo $first_name
Franky

franky ~> full_name="Franky M. Singh"

franky ~> echo $full_name
Franky M. Singh

franky ~> MYVAR-2="2"
bash: MYVAR-2=2: command not found

franky ~> MYVAR1 ="2"
bash: MYVAR1: command not found

franky ~> MYVAR1= "2"
bash: 2: command not found

franky ~> unset MYVAR1 first_name full_name

franky ~> echo $MYVAR1 $first_name $full_name
<--no output-->

franky ~>
```

3.2.2 Exporting variables

A variable created like the ones in the example above is only available to the current shell. It is a local variable: child processes of the current shell will not be aware of this variable. In order to pass variables to a subshell, we need to *export* them using the **export** built-in command. Variables that are exported are referred to as environment variables. Setting and exporting is usually done in one step:

```
export VARNAME="value"
```

A subshell can change variables it inherited from the parent, but the changes made by the child don't affect the parent. This is demonstrated in the example:

```
franky ~> full_name="Franky M. Singh"

franky ~> bash

franky ~> echo $full_name


franky ~> exit

franky ~> export full_name

franky ~> bash

franky ~> echo $full_name
Franky M. Singh

franky ~> export full_name="Charles the Great"

franky ~> echo $full_name
Charles the Great

franky ~> exit

franky ~> echo $full_name
Franky M. Singh

franky ~>
```

When first trying to read the value of full_name in a subshell, it is not there
(**echo** shows a null string). The subshell quits, and full_name is exported in the
parent - a variable can be exported after it has been assigned a value. Then a new
subshell is started, in which the variable exported from the parent is visible. The
variable is changed to hold another name, but the value for this variable in the
parent stays the same.

3.2.3   Reserved variables

There are several variables that have special meaning in Bash scripts. Some of
these *reserved variables* come from the original Bourne shell, while others are specific to Bash.

Bourne shell reserved variables

Bash uses certain shell variables in the same way as the Bourne shell. In some
cases, Bash assigns a default value to the variable. Table 3.1 gives an overview of
these plain shell variables.

Table 3.1: Reserved Bourne shell variables

Variable name	Definition
CDPATH	A colon-separated list of directories used as a search path for the **cd** built-in command.
HOME	The current user's home directory; the default for the **cd** built-in. The value of this variable is also used by tilde expansion.
IFS	A list of characters that separate fields; used when the shell splits words as part of expansion.
MAIL	If this parameter is set to a file name and the `MAILPATH` variable is not set, Bash informs the user of the arrival of mail in the specified file.
MAILPATH	A colon-separated list of file names which the shell periodically checks for new mail.
OPTARG	The value of the last option argument processed by the **getopts** built-in.
OPTIND	The index of the last option argument processed by the **getopts** built-in.
PATH	A colon-separated list of directories in which the shell looks for commands.
PS1	The primary prompt string. The default value is "'\s-\v\$ '".
PS2	The secondary prompt string. The default value is "'> '".

Bash reserved variables

These variables are set or used by Bash, but other shells do not normally treat them specially.

Table 3.2: Reserved Bash variables

Variable name	Definition
auto_resume	This variable controls how the shell interacts with the user and job control.
BASH	The full pathname used to execute the current instance of Bash.
BASH_ENV	If this variable is set when Bash is invoked to execute a shell script, its value is expanded and used as the name of a startup file to read before executing the script.
BASH_VERSION	The version number of the current instance of Bash.
BASH_VERSINFO	A read-only array variable whose members hold version information for this instance of Bash.

COLUMNS	Used by the **select** built-in to determine the terminal width when printing selection lists. Automatically set upon receipt of a *SIGWINCH* signal.
COMP_CWORD	An index into ${COMP_WORDS} of the word containing the current cursor position.
COMP_LINE	The current command line.
COMP_POINT	The index of the current cursor position relative to the beginning of the current command.
COMP_WORDS	An array variable consisting of the individual words in the current command line.
COMPREPLY	An array variable from which Bash reads the possible completions generated by a shell function invoked by the programmable completion facility.
DIRSTACK	An array variable containing the current contents of the directory stack.
EUID	The numeric effective user ID of the current user.
FCEDIT	The editor used as a default by the -e option to the **fc** built-in command.
FIGNORE	A colon-separated list of suffixes to ignore when performing file name completion.
FUNCNAME	The name of any currently-executing shell function.
GLOBIGNORE	A colon-separated list of patterns defining the set of file names to be ignored by file name expansion.
GROUPS	An array variable containing the list of groups of which the current user is a member.
histchars	Up to three characters which control history expansion, quick substitution, and *tokenization*.
HISTCMD	The history number, or index in the history list, of the current command.
HISTCONTROL	Defines whether a command is added to the history file.
HISTFILE	The name of the file to which the command history is saved. The default value is ~/.bash_history.
HISTFILESIZE	The maximum number of lines contained in the history file, defaults to 500.
HISTIGNORE	A colon-separated list of patterns used to decide which command lines should be saved in the history list.
HISTSIZE	The maximum number of commands to remember on the history list, default is 500.
HOSTFILE	Contains the name of a file in the same format as /etc/hosts that should be read when the shell needs to complete a hostname.

HOSTNAME	The name of the current host.
HOSTTYPE	A string describing the machine Bash is running on.
IGNOREEOF	Controls the action of the shell on receipt of an *EOF* character as the sole input.
INPUTRC	The name of the Readline initialization file, overriding the default `/etc/inputrc`.
LANG	Used to determine the locale category for any category not specifically selected with a variable starting with `LC_`.
LC_ALL	This variable overrides the value of `LANG` and any other `LC_`-variable specifying a locale category.
LC_COLLATE	This variable determines the collation order used when sorting the results of file name expansion, and determines the behavior of range expressions, equivalence classes, and collating sequences within file name expansion and pattern matching.
LC_CTYPE	This variable determines the interpretation of characters and the behavior of character classes within file name expansion and pattern matching.
LC_MESSAGES	This variable determines the locale used to translate double-quoted strings preceded by a "$" sign.
LC_NUMERIC	This variable determines the locale category used for number formatting.
LINENO	The line number in the script or shell function currently executing.
LINES	Used by the **select** built-in to determine the column length for printing selection lists.
MACHTYPE	A string that fully describes the system type on which Bash is executing, in the standard GNU CPU-COMPANY-SYSTEM format.
MAILCHECK	How often (in seconds) that the shell should check for mail in the files specified in the `MAILPATH` or `MAIL` variables.
OLDPWD	The previous working directory as set by the **cd** built-in.
OPTERR	If set to the value 1, Bash displays error messages generated by the **getopts** built-in.
OSTYPE	A string describing the operating system Bash is running on.
PIPESTATUS	An array variable containing a list of exit status values from the processes in the most recently executed foreground pipeline (which may contain only a single command).
POSIXLY_CORRECT	If this variable is in the environment when **bash** starts, the shell enters POSIX mode.
PPID	The process ID of the shell's parent process.

PROMPT_COM-MAND	If set, the value is interpreted as a command to execute before the printing of each primary prompt (PS1).
PS3	The value of this variable is used as the prompt for the **select** command. Defaults to "'#? '"
PS4	The value is the prompt printed before the command line is echoed when the -x option is set; defaults to "'+'".
PWD	The current working directory as set by the **cd** built-in command.
RANDOM	Each time this parameter is referenced, a random integer between 0 and 32767 is generated. Assigning a value to this variable seeds the random number generator.
REPLY	The default variable for the **read** built-in.
SECONDS	This variable expands to the number of seconds since the shell was started.
SHELLOPTS	A colon-separated list of enabled shell options.
SHLVL	Incremented by one each time a new instance of Bash is started.
TIMEFORMAT	The value of this parameter is used as a format string specifying how the timing information for pipelines prefixed with the **time** reserved word should be displayed.
TMOUT	If set to a value greater than zero, TMOUT is treated as the default timeout for the **read** built-in. In an interative shell, the value is interpreted as the number of seconds to wait for input after issuing the primary prompt when the shell is interactive. Bash terminates after that number of seconds if input does not arrive.
UID	The numeric, real user ID of the current user.

Check the Bash man, info or doc pages for extended information. Some variables are read-only, some are set automatically and some lose their meaning when set to a different value than the default.

3.2.4 Special parameters

The shell treats several parameters specially. These parameters may only be referenced; assignment to them is not allowed.

Table 3.3: Special bash variables

Character	Definition
$*	Expands to the positional parameters, starting from one. When the expansion occurs within double quotes, it expands to a single word with the value of each parameter separated by the first character of the IFS special variable.
$@	Expands to the positional parameters, starting from one. When the expansion occurs within double quotes, each parameter expands to a separate word.
$#	Expands to the number of positional parameters in decimal.
$?	Expands to the exit status of the most recently executed foreground pipeline.
$-	A hyphen expands to the current option flags as specified upon invocation, by the **set** built-in command, or those set by the shell itself (such as the -i).
$$	Expands to the process ID of the shell.
$!	Expands to the process ID of the most recently executed background (asynchronous) command.
$0	Expands to the name of the shell or shell script.
$_	The underscore variable is set at shell startup and contains the absolute file name of the shell or script being executed as passed in the argument list. Subsequently, it expands to the last argument to the previous command, after expansion. It is also set to the full pathname of each command executed and placed in the environment exported to that command. When checking mail, this parameter holds the name of the mail file.

The positional parameters are the words following the name of a shell script. They are put into the variables $1, $2, $3 and so on. As long as needed, variables are added to an internal array. $# holds the total number of parameters, as is demonstrated with this simple script:

```
#!/bin/bash

# positional.sh
# This script reads 3 positional parameters and prints them out.

POSPAR1="$1"
POSPAR2="$2"
POSPAR3="$3"

echo "$1 is the first positional parameter, \$1."
echo "$2 is the second positional parameter, \$2."
echo "$3 is the third positional parameter, \$3."
echo
echo "The total number of positional parameters is $#."
```

Upon execution one could give any numbers of arguments:

```
franky ~> positional.sh one two three four five
one is the first positional parameter, $1.
two is the second positional parameter, $2.
three is the third positional parameter, $3.

The total number of positional parameters is 5.

franky ~> positional.sh one two
one is the first positional parameter, $1.
two is the second positional parameter, $2.
 is the third positional parameter, $3.

The total number of positional parameters is 2.
```

More on evaluating these parameters is in Chapter 7, "Conditional statements" and Section 9.7.

Some examples on the other special parameters:

```
franky ~> grep dictionary /usr/share/dict/words
dictionary

franky ~> echo $_
/usr/share/dict/words

franky ~> echo $$
10662

franky ~> mozilla &
[1] 11064
```

```
franky ~> echo $!
11064

franky ~> echo $0
bash

franky ~> ls doesnotexist
ls: doesnotexist: No such file or directory

franky ~> echo $?
0

franky ~> echo $?
1

franky ~>
```

User *franky* starts entering the **id**command, which results in the assignment of the
_ variable. The process ID of his shell is 10662. After putting a job in the background, the ! holds the process ID of the backgrounded job. The shell running is
bash. When a mistake is made, ? holds an exit code different from 0 (zero).

3.2.5 Script recycling with variables

Apart from making the script more readable, variables will also enable you to
apply a script more quickly in another environment or for another purpose. Consider the following example, a very simple script that makes a backup of *franky*'s
home directory to a remote server:

```
#!/bin/bash

# This script makes a backup of my home directory.

cd /home

# This creates the archive
tar cf /var/tmp/home_franky.tar franky > /dev/null 2>&1

# First remove the old bzip2 file.  Redirect errors because this generates
# some if the archive does not exist.  Then create a new compressed file.
rm /var/tmp/home_franky.tar.bz2 2> /dev/null
bzip2 /var/tmp/home_franky.tar

# Copy the file to another host - we have ssh keys for making this work
# without intervention.
scp /var/tmp/home_franky.tar.bz2 bordeaux:/opt/backup/franky > /dev/null 2>&1

# Create a timestamp in a logfile.
date > /home/franky/log/home_backup.log
echo backup succeeded > /home/franky/log/home_backup.log
```

First of all, you are more likely to make errors if you name files and directories
manually each time you need them. Secondly, suppose *franky* wants to give this

script to *carol*, then carol will have to do quite some editing before she can use the script to back up her home directory. The same is true if *franky* wants to use this script for backing up other directories. For easy recycling, make all files, directories, usernames, servernames etcetera variable. Thus, you only need to edit a value once, without having to go through the entire script to check where a parameter occurs. This is an example:

```
#!/bin/bash

# This script makes a backup of my home directory.

# Change the values of the variables to make the script work for you:
BACKUPDIR=/home
BACKUPFILES=franky
TARFILE=/var/tmp/home_franky.tar
BZIPFILE=/var/tmp/home_franky.tar.bz2
SERVER=bordeaux
REMOTEDIR=/opt/backup/franky
LOGFILE=/home/franky/log/home_backup.log

cd $BACKUPDIR

# This creates the archive
tar cf $TARFILE $BACKUPFILES > /dev/null 2>&1

# First remove the old bzip2 file. Redirect errors because this generates
# some if the archive does not exist. Then create a new compressed file.
rm $BZIPFILE 2> /dev/null
bzip2 $TARFILE

# Copy the file to another host - we have ssh keys for making this work
# without intervention.
scp $BZIPFILE $SERVER:$REMOTEDIR > /dev/null 2>&1

# Create a timestamp in a logfile.
date > $LOGFILE
echo backup succeeded > $LOGFILE
```

 Large directories and low bandwidth

The above is purely an example that everybody can understand, using a small directory and a host on the same subnet. Depending on your bandwidth, the size of the directory and the location of the remote server, it can take an awful lot of time to make backups using this mechanism. For larger directories and lower bandwidth, use **rsync** to keep the directories at both ends synchronized.

3.3 Quoting characters

3.3.1 Why?

A lot of keys have special meanings in some context or other. Quoting is used to remove the special meaning of characters or words: quotes can disable special treatment for special characters, they can prevent reserved words from being recognized as such and they can disable parameter expansion.

3.3.2 Escape characters

Escape characters are used to remove the special meaning from a single character. A non-quoted backslash, \, is used as an escape character in Bash. It preserves the literal value of the next character that follows, with the exception of *newline*. If a newline character appears immediately after the backslash, it marks the continuation of a line when it is longer that the width of the terminal; the backslash is removed from the input stream and effectively ignored.

```
franky ~> date=20021226

franky ~> echo $date
20021226

franky ~> echo \$date
$date
```

In this example, the variable date is created and set to hold a value. The first **echo** displays the value of the variable, but for the second, the dollar sign is escaped.

3.3.3 Single quotes

Single quotes (") are used to preserve the literal value of each character enclosed within the quotes. A single quote may not occur between single quotes, even when preceded by a backslash.

We continue with the previous example:

```
franky ~> echo \$date
$date
```

3.3.4 Double quotes

Using double quotes the literal value of all characters enclosed is preserved, except for the dollar sign, the backticks (backward single quotes, ") and the backslash.

The dollar sign and the backticks retain their special meaning within the double quotes.

The backslash retains its meaning only when followed by dollar, backtick, double quote, backslash or newline. Within double quotes, the backslashes are removed from the input stream when followed by one of these characters. Backslashes preceding characters that don't have a special meaning are left unmodified for processing by the shell interpreter.

A double quote may be quoted within double quotes by preceding it with a backslash.

```
franky ~> echo "$date"
20021226

franky ~> echo "'date'"
Sun Apr 20 11:22:06 CEST 2003

franky ~> "I'd say: \"Go for it!\""
I'd say: "Go for it!"

franky ~> echo "\"
More input>"

franky ~> echo "\\"
\
```

3.3.5 ANSI-C quoting

Words in the form "$'STRING'" are treated in a special way. The word expands to a string, with backslash-escaped characters replaced as specified by the ANSI-C standard. Backslash escape sequences can be found in the Bash documentation.

3.3.6 Locales

A double-quoted string preceded by a dollar sign will cause the string to be translated according to the current locale. If the current locale is "C" or "POSIX", the dollar sign is ignored. If the string is translated and replaced, the replacement is double-quoted.

3.4 Shell expansion

After the command has been split into *tokens* (see Section 1.4), these tokens or words are expanded or resolved. There are eight kinds of expansion performed, which we will discuss in the next sections, in the order that they are expanded.

After all expansions, quote removal is performed.

3.4.1 Brace expansion

Brace expansion is a mechanism by which arbitrary strings may be generated. Patterns to be brace-expanded take the form of an optional *PREAMBLE*, followed by a series of comma-separated strings between a pair of braces, followed by an optional *POSTSCRIPT*. The preamble is prefixed to each string contained within the braces, and the postscript is then appended to each resulting string, expanding left to right.

Brace expansions may be nested. The results of each expanded string are not sorted; left to right order is preserved:

```
franky ~> echo sp{el,il,al}l
spell spill spall
```

Brace expansion is performed before any other expansions, and any characters special to other expansions are preserved in the result. It is strictly textual. Bash does not apply any syntactic interpretation to the context of the expansion or the text between the braces. To avoid conflicts with parameter expansion, the string "${" is not considered eligible for brace expansion.

A correctly-formed brace expansion must contain unquoted opening and closing braces, and at least one unquoted comma. Any incorrectly formed brace expansion is left unchanged.

3.4.2 Tilde expansion

If a word begins with an unquoted tilde character ("~"), all of the characters up to the first unquoted slash (or all characters, if there is no unquoted slash) are considered a *tilde-prefix*. If none of the characters in the tilde-prefix are quoted, the characters in the tilde-prefix following the tilde are treated as a possible login name. If this login name is the null string, the tilde is replaced with the value of the HOME shell variable. If HOME is unset, the home directory of the user executing the shell is substituted instead. Otherwise, the tilde-prefix is replaced with the home directory associated with the specified login name.

If the tilde-prefix is "~+", the value of the shell variable PWD replaces the tilde-prefix. If the tilde-prefix is "~-", the value of the shell variable OLDPWD, if it is set, is substituted.

If the characters following the tilde in the tilde-prefix consist of a number N, optionally prefixed by a "+" or a "-", the tilde-prefix is replaced with the corresponding element from the directory stack, as it would be displayed by the **dirs** built-in invoked with the characters following tilde in the tilde-prefix as an argument. If the tilde-prefix, without the tilde, consists of a number without a leading "+" or "-", "+" is assumed.

If the login name is invalid, or the tilde expansion fails, the word is left unchanged.

Each variable assignment is checked for unquoted tilde-prefixes immediately following a ":" or "=". In these cases, tilde expansion is also performed. Consequently, one may use file names with tildes in assignments to PATH, MAILPATH, and CDPATH, and the shell assigns the expanded value.

Example:

```
franky ~> export PATH="$PATH:~/testdir"
```

~/testdir will be expanded to $HOME/testdir, so if $HOME is /var/home/franky, the directory /var/home/franky/testdir will be added to the content of the PATH variable.

3.4.3 Shell parameter and variable expansion

The "$" character introduces parameter expansion, command substitution, or arithmetic expansion. The parameter name or symbol to be expanded may be enclosed in braces, which are optional but serve to protect the variable to be expanded from characters immediately following it which could be interpreted as part of the name.

When braces are used, the matching ending brace is the first "}" not escaped by a backslash or within a quoted string, and not within an embedded arithmetic expansion, command substitution, or parameter expansion.

The basic form of parameter expansion is "${PARAMETER}". The value of "PARAMETER" is substituted. The braces are required when "PARAMETER" is a positional parameter with more than one digit, or when "PARAMETER" is followed by a character that is not to be interpreted as part of its name.

If the first character of "PARAMETER" is an exclamation point, Bash uses the value of the variable formed from the rest of "PARAMETER" as the name of the variable; this variable is then expanded and that value is used in the rest of the substitution, rather than the value of "PARAMETER" itself. This is known as *indirect expansion.*

You are certainly familiar with straight parameter expansion, since it happens all the time, even in the simplest of cases, such as the one above or the following:

```
franky ~> echo $SHELL
/bin/bash
```

The following is an example of indirect expansion:

```
franky ~> echo ${!N*}
NNTPPORT NNTPSERVER NPX_PLUGIN_PATH
```

Note that this is not the same as **echo $N***.

The following construct allows for creation of the named variable if it does not yet exist:

```
${VAR:=value}
```

Example:

```
franky ~> echo $FRANKY

franky ~> echo ${FRANKY:=Franky}
Franky
```

Special parameters, among others the positional parameters, may not be assigned this way, however.

We will further discuss the use of the curly braces for treatment of variables in Chapter 10, "More on variables". More information can also be found in the Bash info pages.

3.4.4 Command substitution

Command substitution allows the output of a command to replace the command itself. Command substitution occurs when a command is enclosed like this:

```
$(command)
```

or like this using backticks:

```
`command`
```

Bash performs the expansion by executing COMMAND and replacing the command substitution with the standard output of the command, with any trailing newlines deleted. Embedded newlines are not deleted, but they may be removed during word splitting.

```
franky ~> echo 'date'
Thu Feb 6 10:06:20 CET 2003
```

When the old-style backquoted form of substitution is used, backslash retains its literal meaning except when followed by "$", """, or "\". The first backticks not preceded by a backslash terminates the command substitution. When using the "$(COMMAND)" form, all characters between the parentheses make up the command; none are treated specially.

Command substitutions may be nested. To nest when using the backquoted form, escape the inner backticks with backslashes.

If the substitution appears within double quotes, word splitting and file name expansion are not performed on the results.

3.4.5   Arithmetic expansion

Arithmetic expansion allows the evaluation of an arithmetic expression and the substitution of the result. The format for arithmetic expansion is:

```
$(( EXPRESSION ))
```

The expression is treated as if it were within double quotes, but a double quote inside the parentheses is not treated specially. All tokens in the expression undergo parameter expansion, command substitution, and quote removal. Arithmetic substitutions may be nested.

Evaluation of arithmetic expressions is done in fixed-width integers with no check for overflow - although division by zero is trapped and recognized as an error. The operators are the same as in the C programming language. In order of decreasing precedence, the list looks like this:

Table 3.4: Arithmetic operators

Operator	Meaning
VAR++ and VAR–	variable post-increment and post-decrement
++VAR and –VAR	variable pre-increment and pre-decrement
- and +	unary minus and plus
! and ~	logical and bitwise negation
**	exponentiation
*, / and %	multiplication, division, remainder
+ and -	addition, subtraction
<< and >>	left and right bitwise shifts
<=, >=, < and >	comparison operators

== and !==	equality and inequality
&	bitwise AND
^	bitwise exclusive OR
|	bitwise OR
&&	logical AND
||	logical OR
expr ? expr : expr	conditional evaluation
=, *=, /=, %=, +=, -=, <<=, >>=, &=, ^= and |=	assignments
,	separator between expressions

Shell variables are allowed as operands; parameter expansion is performed before the expression is evaluated. Within an expression, shell variables may also be referenced by name without using the parameter expansion syntax. The value of a variable is evaluated as an arithmetic expression when it is referenced. A shell variable need not have its integer attribute turned on to be used in an expression.

Constants with a leading 0 (zero) are interpreted as octal numbers. A leading "0x" or "0X" denotes hexadecimal. Otherwise, numbers take the form "[BASE'#']N", where "BASE" is a decimal number between 2 and 64 representing the arithmetic base, and N is a number in that base. If "BASE'#'" is omitted, then base 10 is used. The digits greater than 9 are represented by the lowercase letters, the uppercase letters, "@", and "_", in that order. If "BASE" is less than or equal to 36, lowercase and uppercase letters may be used interchangably to represent numbers between 10 and 35.

Operators are evaluated in order of precedence. Sub-expressions in parentheses are evaluated first and may override the precedence rules above.

Wherever possible, Bash users should try to use the syntax with angular brackets:

```
$[ EXPRESSION ]
```

However, this will only calculate the result of *EXPRESSION*, and do no tests:

```
franky ~> echo $[365*24]
8760
```

See Section 7.1.1, among others, for practical examples in scripts.

3.4.6   Process substitution

Process substitution is supported on systems that support named pipes (FIFOs) or the /dev/fd method of naming open files. It takes the form of

> <(LIST)

or

> >(LIST)

The process LIST is run with its input or output connected to a FIFO or some file in /dev/fd. The name of this file is passed as an argument to the current command as the result of the expansion. If the ">(LIST)" form is used, writing to the file will provide input for LIST. If the "<(LIST)" form is used, the file passed as an argument should be read to obtain the output of LIST. Note that no space may appear between the < or > signs and the left parenthesis, otherwise the construct would be interpreted as a redirection.

When available, process substitution is performed simultaneously with parameter and variable expansion, command substitution, and arithmetic expansion.

More information in Section 8.2.2.

3.4.7 Word splitting

The shell scans the results of parameter expansion, command substitution, and arithmetic expansion that did not occur within double quotes for word splitting.

The shell treats each character of $IFS as a delimiter, and splits the results of the other expansions into words on these characters. If IF is unset, or its value is exactly "'<space><tab><newline>'", the default, then any sequence of IFS characters serves to delimit words. If IFS has a value other than the default, then sequences of the whitespace characters "space" and "Tab" are ignored at the beginning and end of the word, as long as the whitespace character is in the value of IFS (an IFS whitespace character). Any character in IFS that is not IFS whitespace, along with any adjacent IF whitespace characters, delimits a field. A sequence of IFS whitespace characters is also treated as a delimiter. If the value of IFS is null, no word splitting occurs.

Explicit null arguments ("""" or """") are retained. Unquoted implicit null arguments, resulting from the expansion of parameters that have no values, are removed. If a parameter with no value is expanded within double quotes, a null argument results and is retained.

 Expansion and word splitting

If no expansion occurs, no splitting is performed.

3.4.8 File name expansion

After word splitting, unless the -f option has been set (see Section 2.3.1), Bash scans each word for the characters "*", "?", and "[". If one of these characters appears, then the word is regarded as a *PATTERN*, and replaced with an alphabetically sorted list of file names matching the pattern. If no matching file names are found, and the shell option `nullglob` is disabled, the word is left unchanged. If the `nullglob` option is set, and no matches are found, the word is removed. If the shell option `nocaseglob` is enabled, the match is performed without regard to the case of alphabetic characters.

When a pattern is used for file name generation, the character "." at the start of a file name or immediately following a slash must be matched explicitly, unless the shell option `dotglob` is set. When matching a file name, the slash character must always be matched explicitly. In other cases, the "." character is not treated specially.

The `GLOBIGNORE` shell variable may be used to restrict the set of file names matching a pattern. If `GLOBIGNORE` is set, each matching file name that also matches one of the patterns in `GLOBIGNORE` is removed from the list of matches. The file names . and .. are always ignored, even when `GLOBIGNORE` is set. However, setting `GLOBIGNORE` has the effect of enabling the `dotglob` shell option, so all other file names beginning with a "." will match. To get the old behavior of ignoring file names beginning with a ".", make ".*" one of the patterns in `GLOBIGNORE`. The `dotglob` option is disabled when `GLOBIGNORE` is unset.

3.5 Aliases

3.5.1 What are aliases?

An alias allows a string to be substituted for a word when it is used as the first word of a simple command. The shell maintains a list of aliases that may be set and unset with the **alias** and **unalias** built-in commands. Issue the **alias** without options to display a list of aliases known to the current shell.

```
franky: ~> alias
alias ..='cd ..'
alias ...='cd ../..'
alias ....='cd ../../..'
alias PAGER='less -r'
alias Txterm='export TERM=xterm'
alias XARGS='xargs -r'
alias cdrecord='cdrecord -dev 0,0,0 -speed=8'
alias e='vi'
alias egrep='grep -E'
alias ewformat='fdformat -n /dev/fd0u1743; ewfsck'
alias fgrep='grep -F'
alias ftp='ncftp -d15'
alias h='history 10'
alias fformat='fdformat /dev/fd0H1440'
alias j='jobs -l'
alias ksane='setterm -reset'
alias ls='ls -F --color=auto'
alias m='less'
alias md='mkdir'
alias od='od -Ax -ta -txC'
alias p='pstree -p'
alias ping='ping -vc1'
alias sb='ssh blubber'
alias sl='ls'
alias ss='ssh octarine'
alias sss='ssh -C server1.us.soti.org'
alias sssu='ssh -C -l root server1.us.soti.org'
alias tar='gtar'
alias tmp='cd /tmp'
alias unaliasall='unalias -a'
alias vi='eval `resize`;vi'
alias vt100='export TERM=vt100'
alias which='type'
alias xt='xterm -bg black -fg white &'

franky ~>
```

Aliases are useful for specifying the default version of a command that exists in several versions on your system, or to specify default options to a command. Another use for aliases is for correcting incorrect spelling.

The first word of each simple command, if unquoted, is checked to see if it has an alias. If so, that word is replaced by the text of the alias. The alias name and the replacement text may contain any valid shell input, including shell metacharacters, with the exception that the alias name may not contain "=". The first word of the replacement text is tested for aliases, but a word that is identical to an alias being expanded is not expanded a second time. This means that one may alias **ls** to **ls -F**, for instance, and Bash will not try to recursively expand the replacement text. If the last character of the alias value is a space or tab character, then the next command word following the alias is also checked for alias expansion.

Aliases are not expanded when the shell is not interactive, unless the expand_-aliases option is set using the **shopt** shell built-in.

3.5.2 Creating and removing aliases

Aliases are created using the **alias** shell built-in. For permanent use, enter the **alias** in one of your shell initialization files; if you just enter the alias on the command line, it is only recognized within the current shell.

```
franky ~> alias dh='df -h'

franky ~> dh
Filesystem              Size  Used Avail Use% Mounted on
/dev/hda7               1.3G  272M 1018M  22% /
/dev/hda1               121M  9.4M  105M   9% /boot
/dev/hda2                13G  8.7G  3.7G  70% /home
/dev/hda3                13G  5.3G  7.1G  43% /opt
none                    243M     0  243M   0% /dev/shm
/dev/hda6               3.9G  3.2G  572M  85% /usr
/dev/hda5               5.2G  4.3G  725M  86% /var

franky ~> unalias dh

franky ~> dh
bash: dh: command not found

franky ~>
```

Bash always reads at least one complete line of input before executing any of the commands on that line. Aliases are expanded when a command is read, not when it is executed. Therefore, an alias definition appearing on the same line as another command does not take effect until the next line of input is read. The commands following the alias definition on that line are not affected by the new alias. This behavior is also an issue when functions are executed. Aliases are expanded when a function definition is read, not when the function is executed, because a function definition is itself a compound command. As a consequence, aliases defined in a function are not available until after that function is executed. To be safe, always put alias definitions on a separate line, and do not use **alias** in compound commands.

Aliases are not inherited by child processes. Bourne shell (**sh**) does not recognize aliases.

More about functions is in Chapter 11, "Functions".

 Functions are faster

> Aliases are looked up after functions, so they are resolved more slowly. While aliases are easier to understand, shell functions are preferred over aliases for almost every purpose.

3.6 More Bash options

We already discussed a couple of Bash options that are useful for debugging your scripts. In this section, we will take a more in-depth view of the Bash options.

Use the -o option to **set** to display all shell options:

```
willy:~> set -o
allexport             off
braceexpand           on
emacs                 on
errexit               off
hashall               on
histexpand            on
history               on
ignoreeof             off
interactive-comments  on
keyword               off
monitor               on
noclobber             off
noexec                off
noglob                off
nolog                 off
notify                off
nounset               off
onecmd                off
physical              off
posix                 off
privileged            off
verbose               off
vi                    off
xtrace                off
```

See the Bash Info pages, section **Shell Built-in Commands → The Set Built-in** for a description of each option. A lot of options have one-character shorthands: the xtrace option, for instance, is equal to specifying **set -x**.

3.6.1 Changing options

Shell options can either be set different from the default upon calling the shell, or be set during shell operation. They may also be included in the shell resource configuration files.

The following command executes a script in POSIX-compatible mode:

```
willy:~/scripts> bash --posix script.sh
```

For changing the current environment temporarily, or for use in a script, we would rather use **set**. Use - (dash) for enabling an option, + for disabling:

```
willy:~/test> set -o noclobber

willy:~/test> touch test

willy:~/test> date > test
bash: test: cannot overwrite existing file

willy:~/test> set +o noclobber

willy:~/test> date > test
```

The above example demonstrates the noclobber option, which prevents existing files from being overwritten by redirection operations. The same goes for one-character options, for instance -u, which will treat unset variables as an error when set, and exits a non-interactive shell upon encountering such errors:

```
willy:~> echo $VAR

willy:~> set -u

willy:~> echo $VAR
bash: VAR: unbound variable
```

This option is also useful for detecting incorrect content assignment to variables: the same error will also occur, for instance, when assigning a character string to a variable that was declared explicitly as one holding only integer values.

One last example follows, demonstrating the noglob option, which prevents special characters from being expanded:

```
willy:~/testdir> set -o noglob

willy:~/testdir> touch *

willy:~/testdir> ls -l *
-rw-rw-r--    1 willy    willy       0 Feb 27 13:37 *
```

3.7 Summary

The Bash environment can be configured globally and on a per user basis. Various configuration files are used to fine-tune the behavior of the shell.

These files contain shell options, settings for variables, function definitions and various other building blocks for creating ourselves a cosy environment.

Except for the reserved Bourne shell, Bash and special parameters, variable names can be chosen more or less freely.

Because a lot of characters have double or even triple meanings, depending on the environment, Bash uses a system of quoting to take away special meaning from one or multiple characters when special treatment is not wanted.

Bash uses various methods of expanding command line entries in order to determine which commands to execute.

3.8 Exercises

For this exercise, you will need to read the **useradd** man pages, because we are going to use the /etc/skel directory to hold default shell configuration files, which are copied to the home directory of each newly added user.

First we will do some general exercises on setting and displaying variables. Don't forget to **chmod** your scripts!

1. Create 3 variables, VAR1, VAR2 and VAR3; initialize them to hold the values "thirteen", "13" and "Happy Birthday" respectively.

2. Display the values of all three variables.

3. Are these local or global variables?

4. Remove VAR3.

5. Can you see the two remaining variables in a new terminal window?

6. Edit /etc/profile so that all users are greeted upon login (test this).

7. For the *root* account, set the prompt to something like "Danger!! root is doing stuff in \w", preferably in a bright color such as red or pink or in reverse video mode.

8. Make sure that newly created users also get a nice personalized prompt which informs them on which system in which directory they are working. Test your changes by adding a new user and logging in as that user.

9. Write a script in which you assign two integer values to two variables. The script should calculate the surface of a rectangle which has these proportions. It should be aired with comments and generate elegant output.

Chapter 4

Regular expressions

In this chapter we discuss:

- *Using regular expressions*
- *Regular expression metacharacters*
- *Finding patterns in files or output*
- *Character ranges and classes in Bash*

4.1 Regular expressions

A *regular expression* is a pattern that describes a set of strings. Regular expressions are constructed analogously to arithmetic expressions by using various operators to combine smaller expressions.

The fundamental building blocks are the regular expressions that match a single character. Most characters, including all letters and digits, are regular expressions that match themselves. Any metacharacter with special meaning may be quoted by preceding it with a backslash.

4.1.1 Regular expression metacharacters

A regular expression may be followed by one of several repetition operators (metacharacters):

Table 4.1: Regular expression operators

Operator	Effect
.	Matches any single character.
?	The preceding item is optional and will be matched, at most, once.
*	The preceding item will be matched zero or more times.
+	The preceding item will be matched one or more times.
{N}	The preceding item is matched exactly N times.
{N,}	The preceding item is matched N or more times.
{N,M}	The preceding item is matched at least N times, but not more than M times.
-	represents the range if it's not first or last in a list or the ending point of a range in a list.
^	Matches the empty string at the beginning of a line; also represents the characters not in the range of a list.
$	Matches the empty string at the end of a line.
\b	Matches the empty string at the edge of a word.
\B	Matches the empty string provided it's not at the edge of a word.
\<	Match the empty string at the beginning of word.
\>	Match the empty string at the end of word.

Two regular expressions may be concatenated; the resulting regular expression matches any string formed by concatenating two substrings that respectively match the concatenated subexpressions.

Two regular expressions may be joined by the infix operator "|"; the resulting regular expression matches any string matching either subexpression.

Repetition takes precedence over concatenation, which in turn takes precedence over alternation. A whole subexpression may be enclosed in parentheses to override these precedence rules.

4.1.2 Basic versus extended regular expressions

In basic regular expressions the metacharacters "?", "+", "{", "|", "(", and ")" lose their special meaning; instead use the backslashed versions "\?", "\+", "\{", "\|", "\(", and "\)".

Check in your system documentation whether commands using regular expressions support extended expressions.

4.2 Examples using grep

grep searches the input files for lines containing a match to a given pattern list. When it finds a match in a line, it copies the line to standard output (by default), or whatever other sort of output you have requested with options.

Though **grep** expects to do the matching on text, it has no limits on input line length other than available memory, and it can match arbitrary characters within a line. If the final byte of an input file is not a *newline*, **grep** silently supplies one. Since newline is also a separator for the list of patterns, there is no way to match newline characters in a text.

Some examples:

```
cathy ~> grep root /etc/passwd
root:x:0:0:root:/root:/bin/bash
operator:x:11:0:operator:/root:/sbin/nologin

cathy ~> grep -n root /etc/passwd
1:root:x:0:0:root:/root:/bin/bash
12:operator:x:11:0:operator:/root:/sbin/nologin

cathy ~> grep -v bash /etc/passwd | grep -v nologin
sync:x:5:0:sync:/sbin:/bin/sync
shutdown:x:6:0:shutdown:/sbin:/sbin/shutdown
halt:x:7:0:halt:/sbin:/sbin/halt
news:x:9:13:news:/var/spool/news:
mailnull:x:47:47::/var/spool/mqueue:/dev/null
xfs:x:43:43:X Font Server:/etc/X11/fs:/bin/false
rpc:x:32:32:Portmapper RPC user:/:/bin/false
nscd:x:28:28:NSCD Daemon:/:/bin/false
named:x:25:25:Named:/var/named:/bin/false
squid:x:23:23::/var/spool/squid:/dev/null
ldap:x:55:55:LDAP User:/var/lib/ldap:/bin/false
apache:x:48:48:Apache:/var/www:/bin/false
```

```
cathy ~> grep -c false /etc/passwd
7

cathy ~> grep -i ps ~/.bash* | grep -v history
/home/cathy/.bashrc:PS1="\[\033[1;44m\]$USER is in \w\[\033[0m\] "
```

With the first command, user *cathy* displays the lines from /etc/passwd containing the string *root*.

Then she displays the line numbers containing this search string.

With the third command she checks which users are not using **bash**, but accounts with the **nologin** shell are not displayed.

Then she counts the number of accounts that have /bin/false as the shell.

The last command displays the lines from all the files in her home directory starting with ~/.bash, excluding matches containing history, so as to exclude matches from ~/.bash_history which might contain the same string, in upper or lower cases.

Now let's see what else we can do with grep, using regular expressions.

4.2.1   Grep and regular expressions

 If you are not on Linux

> We use GNU **grep** in these examples, which supports extended regular expressions. GNU **grep** is the default on Linux systems. If you are working on proprietary systems, check with the -V option which version you are using. GNU **grep** can be downloaded from <http://gnu.org/directory/>.

Line and word anchors

From the previous example, we now exclusively want to display lines starting with the string "root":

```
cathy ~> grep ^root /etc/passwd
root:x:0:0:root:/root:/bin/bash
```

If we want to see which accounts have no shell assigned whatsoever, we search for lines ending in ":":

```
cathy ~> grep :$ /etc/passwd
news:x:9:13:news:/var/spool/news:
```

To check that PATH is exported in ~/.bashrc, first select "export" lines and then search for lines starting with the string "PATH", so as not to display MANPATH and other possible paths:

```
cathy ~> grep export ~/.bashrc | grep '\<PATH'
export PATH="/bin:/usr/lib/mh:/lib:/usr/bin:/usr/local/bin:/usr/ucb:/usr/dbin:$PATH"
```

Similarly, \> matches the end of a word.

If you want to find a string that is a separate word (enclosed by spaces), it is better use the -w, as in this example where we are displaying information for the root partition:

```
cathy ~> grep -w / /etc/fstab
LABEL=/                       /                    ext3     defaults      1 1
```

If this option is not used, all the lines from the file system table will be displayed.

Character classes

A *bracket expression* is a list of characters enclosed by "[" and "]". It matches any single character in that list; if the first character of the list is the caret, "^", then it matches any character NOT in the list. For example, the regular expression "[0123456789]" matches any single digit.

Within a bracket expression, a *range expression* consists of two characters separated by a hyphen. It matches any single character that sorts between the two characters, inclusive, using the locale's collating sequence and character set. For example, in the default C locale, "[a-d]" is equivalent to "[abcd]". Many locales sort characters in dictionary order, and in these locales "[a-d]" is typically not equivalent to "[abcd]"; it might be equivalent to "[aBbCcDd]", for example. To obtain the traditional interpretation of bracket expressions, you can use the C locale by setting the LC_ALL environment variable to the value "C".

Finally, certain named classes of characters are predefined within bracket expressions. See the **grep** man or info pages for more information about these predefined expressions.

```
cathy ~> grep [yf] /etc/group
sys:x:3:root,bin,adm
tty:x:5:
mail:x:12:mail,postfix
ftp:x:50:
nobody:x:99:
floppy:x:19:
xfs:x:43:
nfsnobody:x:65534:
postfix:x:89:

cathy ~> ls *[1-9].xml
app1.xml   chap1.xml   chap2.xml   chap3.xml   chap4.xml
```

In the example, all the lines containing either a "y" or "f" character are first displayed, followed by an example of using a range with the **ls** command.

Wildcards

Use the "." for a single character match. If you want to get a list of all five-character English dictionary words starting with "c" and ending in "h" (handy for solving crosswords):

```
cathy ~> grep '\<c...h\>' /usr/share/dict/words
catch
clash
cloth
coach
couch
cough
crash
crush
```

If you want to display lines containing the literal dot character, use the -F option to **grep**.

For matching multiple characters, use the asterisk. This example selects all words starting with "c" and ending in "h" from the system's dictionary:

```
cathy ~> grep '\<c.*h\>' /usr/share/dict/words
caliph
cash
catch
cheesecloth
cheetah
--output omitted--
```

If you want to find the literal asterisk character in a file or output, use **grep -F**:

```
cathy ~> grep * /etc/profile

cathy ~> grep -F '*' /etc/profile
for i in /etc/profile.d/*.sh ; do
```

4.3 Pattern matching using Bash features

Apart from **grep** and regular expressions, there's a good deal of pattern matching that you can do directly in the shell, without having to use an external program.

4.3.1 Character ranges

As you already know, the asterisk (*) and the question mark (?) match any string or any single character, respectively. Quote these special characters to match them literally:

```
cathy ~> touch "*"

cathy ~> ls "*"
*
```

But you can also use the square braces to match any enclosed character or range of characters, if pairs of characters are separated by a hyphen. An example:

```
cathy ~> ls -ld [a-cx-z]*
drwxr-xr-x    2 cathy      cathy          4096 Jul 20  2002 app-defaults/
drwxrwxr-x    4 cathy      cathy          4096 May 25  2002 arabic/
drwxrwxr-x    2 cathy      cathy          4096 Mar  4 18:30 bin/
drwxr-xr-x    7 cathy      cathy          4096 Sep  2  2001 crossover/
drwxrwxr-x    3 cathy      cathy          4096 Mar 22  2002 xml/
```

This lists all files in *cathy*'s home directory, starting with "a", "b", "c", "x", "y" or "z".

If the first character within the braces is "!" or "^", any character not enclosed will be matched. To match the dash ("-"), include it as the first or last character in the set. The sorting depends on the current locale and of the value of the LC_-COLLATE variable, if it is set. Mind that other locales might interpret "[a-cx-z]" as "[aBbCcXxYyZz]" if sorting is done in dictionary order. If you want to be sure to have the traditional interpretation of ranges, force this behavior by setting LC_-COLLATE or LC_ALL to "C".

4.3.2 Character classes

Character classes can be specified within the square braces, using the syntax **[:CLASS:]**, where CLASS is defined in the POSIX standard and has one of the

values

"alnum", "alpha", "ascii", "blank", "cntrl", "digit", "graph", "lower", "print", "punct", "space", "upper", "word" or "xdigit".

Some examples:

```
cathy ~> ls -ld [[:digit:]]*
drwxrwxr-x    2 cathy    cathy           4096 Apr 20 13:45 2/

cathy ~> ls -ld [[:upper:]]*
drwxrwxr--    3 cathy    cathy           4096 Sep 30  2001 Nautilus/
drwxrwxr-x    4 cathy    cathy           4096 Jul 11  2002 OpenOffice.org1.0/
-rw-rw-r--    1 cathy    cathy         997376 Apr 18 15:39 Schedule.sdc
```

When the `extglob` shell option is enabled (using the **shopt** built-in), several extended pattern matching operators are recognized. Read more in the Bash info pages, section **Basic shell features** → **Shell Expansions** → **Filename Expansion** → **Pattern Matching**.

4.4 Summary

Regular expressions are powerful tools for selecting particular lines from files or output. A lot of UNIX commands use regular expressions: **vim**, **perl**, the PostgreSQL database and so on. They can be made available in any language or application using external libraries, and they even found their way to non-UNIX systems. For instance, regular expressions are used in the Excell spreadsheet that comes with the MicroSoft Windows Office suite. In this chapter we got the feel of the **grep** command, which is indispensable in any UNIX environment.

 Note

The **grep** command can do much more than the few tasks we discussed here; we only used it as an example for regular expressions. The GNU **grep** version comes with plenty of documentation, which you are strongly advised to read!

Bash has built-in features for matching patterns and can recognize character classes and ranges.

4.5 Exercises

These exercises will help you master regular expressions.

1. Display a list of all the users on your system who log in with the Bash shell as a default.

2. From the /etc/group directory, display all lines starting with the string "daemon".

3. Print all the lines from the same file that don't contain the string.

4. Display localhost information from the /etc/hosts file, display the line number(s) matching the search string and count the number of occurrences of the string.

5. Display a list of /usr/share/doc subdirectories containing information about shells.

6. How many README files do these subdirectories contain? Don't count anything in the form of "README.a_string".

7. Make a list of files in your home directory that were changed less that 10 hours ago, using **grep**, but leave out directories.

8. Put these commands in a shell script that will generate comprehensible output.

9. Can you find an alternative for **wc -l**, using **grep**?

10. Using the file system table (/etc/fstab for instance), list local disk devices.

11. Make a script that checks whether a user exists in /etc/passwd. For now, you can specify the user name in the script, you don't have to work with arguments and conditionals at this stage.

12. Display configuration files in /etc that contain numbers in their names.

Chapter 5

The GNU sed stream editor

At the end of this chapter you will know about the following topics:

- *What is **sed**?*
- *Interactive use of **sed***
- *Regular expressions and stream editing*
- *Using **sed** commands in scripts*

 This is an introduction

*These explanations are far from complete and certainly not meant to be used as the definite user manual for **sed**. This chapter is only included in order to show some more interesting topics in the next chapters, and because every power user should have a basic knowledge of things that can be done with this editor.*

*For detailed information, refer to the **sed** info and man pages.*

5.1 Introduction

A Stream EDitor is used to perform basic transformations on text read from a file or a pipe. The result is sent to standard output. The syntax for the **sed** command has no output file specification, but results can be saved to a file using output redirection. The editor does not modify the original input.

What distinguishes **sed** from other editors, such as **vi** and **ed**, is its ability to filter text that it gets from a pipeline feed. You do not need to interact with the editor while it is running; that is why **sed** is sometimes called a *batch editor*. This feature allows use of editing commands in scripts, greatly easing repetitive editing tasks. When facing replacement of text in a large number of files, **sed** is a great help.

5.1.1 sed commands

The **sed** program can perform text pattern substitutions and deletions using regular expressions, like the ones used with the **grep** command; see Section 4.2.

The editing commands are similar to the ones used in the **vi** editor:

Table 5.1: Sed editing commands

Command	Result
a\	Append text below current line.
c\	Change text in the current line with new text.
d	Delete text.
i\	Insert text above current line.
p	Print text.
r	Read a file.
s	Search and replace text.
w	Write to a file.

Apart from editing commands, you can give options to **sed**. An overview is in the table below:

Table 5.2: Sed options

Option	Effect
-e SCRIPT	Add the commands in SCRIPT to the set of commands to be run while processing the input.
-f	Add the commands contained in the file SCRIPT-FILE to the set of commands to be run while processing the input.
-n	Silent mode.

-v	Print version information and exit.

The **sed** info pages contain more information; we only list the most frequently used commands and options here.

5.2 Interactive editing

In this section, we examine several common tasks you may want to do *interactively* with sed, as opposed to running the tasks to completion without human intervention.

5.2.1 Printing lines containing a pattern

This is something you can do with **grep**, of course, but you can't do a "find and replace" using that command. This is just to get you started.

Here is our example text file:

```
sandy ~> cat -n example
     1  This is the first line of an example text.
     2  It is a text with erors.
     3  Lots of erors.
     4  So much erors, all these erors are making me sick.
     5  This is a line not containing any errors.
     6  This is the last line.

sandy ~>
```

We want **sed** to find all the lines containing our search pattern, in this case "erors". We use the **p** to obtain the result:

```
sandy ~> sed  '/erors/p' example
This is the first line of an example text.
It is a text with erors.
It is a text with erors.
Lots of erors.
Lots of erors.
So much erors, all these erors are making me sick.
So much erors, all these erors are making me sick.
This is a line not containing any errors.
This is the last line.

sandy ~>
```

As you notice, **sed** prints the entire file, but the lines containing the search string are printed twice. This is not what we want. In order to only print those lines matching our pattern, use the -n option:

```
sandy ~> sed -n '/erors/p' example
It is a text with erors.
Lots of erors.
So much erors, all these erors are making me sick.

sandy ~>
```

5.2.2 Deleting lines of input containing a pattern

We use the same example text file. Now we only want to see the lines *not* containing the search string:

```
sandy ~> sed '/erors/d' example
This is the first line of an example text.
This is a line not containing any errors.
This is the last line.

sandy ~>
```

The **d** command results in excluding lines from being displayed.

Matching lines starting with a given pattern and ending in a second pattern are showed like this:

```
sandy ~> sed -n '/^This.*errors.$/p' example
This is a line not containing any errors.

sandy ~>
```

5.2.3 Ranges of lines

This time we want to take out the lines containing the errors. In the example these are lines 2 to 4. Specify this range to address, together with the **d** command:

```
sandy ~> sed '2,4d' example
This is the first line of an example text.
This is a line not containing any errors.
This is the last line.

sandy ~>
```

To print the file starting from a certain line until the end of the file, use a command similar to this:

```
sandy ~> sed '3,$d' example
This is the first line of an example text.
It is a text with erors.

sandy ~>
```

This only prints the first two lines of the example file.

The following command prints the first line containing the pattern "a text", up to and including the next line containing the pattern "a line":

```
sandy ~> sed -n '/a text/,/This/p' example
It is a text with erors.
Lots of erors.
So much erors, all these erors are making me sick.
This is a line not containing any errors.

sandy ~>
```

5.2.4   Find and replace with sed

In the example file, we will now search and replace the errors instead of only (de)selecting the lines containing the search string.

```
sandy ~> sed 's/erors/errors/' example
This is the first line of an example text.
It is a text with errors.
Lots of errors.
So much errors, all these erors are making me sick.
This is a line not containing any errors.
This is the last line.

sandy ~>
```

As you can see, this is not exactly the desired effect: in line 4, only the first occurrence of the search string has been replaced, and there is still an 'eror' left. Use the **g** command to indicate to **sed** that it should examine the entire line instead of stopping at the first occurrence of your string:

```
sandy ~> sed 's/erors/errors/g' example
This is the first line of an example text.
It is a text with errors.
Lots of errors.
So much errors, all these errors are making me sick.
This is a line not containing any errors.
This is the last line.

sandy ~>
```

To insert a string at the beginning of each line of a file, for instance for quoting:

```
sandy ~> sed 's/^/> /' example
> This is the first line of an example text.
> It is a text with erors.
> Lots of erors.
> So much erors, all these erors are making me sick.
> This is a line not containing any errors.
> This is the last line.

sandy ~>
```

Insert some string at the end of each line:

```
sandy ~> sed 's/$/EOL/' example
This is the first line of an example text.EOL
It is a text with erors.EOL
Lots of erors.EOL
So much erors, all these erors are making me sick.EOL
This is a line not containing any errors.EOL
This is the last line.EOL

sandy ~>
```

Multiple find and replace commands are separated with individual -e options:

```
sandy ~> sed -e 's/erors/errors/g' -e 's/last/final/g' example
This is the first line of an example text.
It is a text with errors.
Lots of errors.
So much errors, all these errors are making me sick.
This is a line not containing any errors.
This is the final line.

sandy ~>
```

Keep in mind that by default **sed** prints its results to the standard output, most likely your terminal window. If you want to save the output to a file, redirect it:

```
sed option 'cmd/expression' infile > outfile
```

 **More examples**

Plenty of **sed** examples can be found in the startup scripts for your machine, which are usually in /etc/init.d or /etc/rc.d/init.d. Change into the directory containing the initscripts on your system and issue the following command:

```
grep sed *
```

5.3 Non-interactive editing

There are several ways to run **sed** without any human interaction.

5.3.1 Reading sed commands from a file

Multiple **sed** commands can be put in a file and executed using the -f option. When creating such a file, make sure that:

- No trailing white spaces exist at the end of lines.
- No quotes are used.
- When entering text to add or replace, all except the last line end in a backslash.

5.3.2 Writing output files

Writing output is done using the output redirection operator >. This is an example script used to create very simple HTML files from plain text files.

```
sandy ~> cat script.sed
1i\
<html>\
<head><title>sed generated html</title></head>\
<body bgcolor="#ffffff">\
<pre>
$a\
</pre>\
</body>\
</html>

sandy ~> cat txt2html.sh
#!/bin/bash

# This is a simple script that you can use for converting text into HTML.
# First we take out all newline characters, so that the appending only
# happens once, then we replace the newlines.
```

```
echo "converting $1..."

SCRIPT="/home/sandy/scripts/script.sed"
NAME="$1"
TEMPFILE="/var/tmp/sed.$PID.tmp"
sed "s/\n/^M/" $1 | sed -f $SCRIPT | sed "s/^M/\n/" > $TEMPFILE
mv $TEMPFILE $NAME

echo "done."

sandy ~>
```

$1 holds the first argument to a given command, in this case the name of the file to convert:

```
sandy ~> cat test
line1
line2
line3
```

More on positional parameters in Chapter 7, "Conditional statements".

```
sandy ~> txt2html.sh test
converting test...
done.

sandy ~> cat test
<html>
<head><title>sed generated html</title></head>
<body bgcolor="#ffffff">
<pre>
line1
line2
line3
</pre>
</body>
</html>

sandy ~>
```

This is not really how it is done; this example just demonstrates **sed** capabilities. See Section 6.3 for a more decent solution to this problem, using **awk** *BEGIN* and *END* constructs.

 Easy sed

Advanced editors, supporting syntax highlighting, can recognize **sed** syntax. This can be a great help if you tend to forget backslashes and such.

5.4 Summary

The **sed** stream editor is a powerful command line tool, which can handle streams of data: it can take input lines from a pipe. This makes it fit for non-interactive use. The **sed** editor uses **vi**-like commands and accepts regular expressions.

The **sed** tool can read commands from the command line or from a script. It is often used to perform find-and-replace actions on lines containing a pattern.

5.5 Exercises

These exercises are meant to further demonstrate what **sed** can do.

1. Print a list of files in your `scripts` directory, ending in ".sh". Mind that you might have to unalias **ls**. Put the result in a temporary file.

2. Make a list of files in /usr/bin that have the letter "a" as the second character. Put the result in a temporary file.

3. Delete the first 3 lines of each temporary file.

4. Print to standard output only the lines containing the pattern "an".

5. Create a file holding **sed** commands to perform the previous two tasks. Add an extra command to this file that adds a string like "*** This might have something to do with man and man pages ***" in the line preceding every occurence of the string "man". Check the results.

6. A long listing of the root directory, /, is used for input. Create a file holding **sed** commands that check for symbolic links and plain files. If a file is a symbolic link, precede it with a line like "–This is a symlink–". If the file is a plain file, add a string on the same line, adding a comment like "<– this is a plain file".

7. Create a script that shows lines containing trailing white spaces from a file. This script should use a **sed** script and show sensible information to the user.

Chapter 6

The GNU awk programming language

In this chapter we will discuss:

- *What is gawk?*
- *Using gawk commands on the command line*
- *How to format text with gawk*
- *How gawk uses regular expressions*
- *Gawk in scripts*
- *Gawk and variables*

 To make it more fun

*As with **sed**, entire books have been written about various versions of **awk**. This introduction is far from complete and is only intended for understanding examples in the following chapters. For more information, best start with the documentation that comes with GNU awk: "GAWK: Effective AWK Programming: A User's Guide for GNU Awk".*

6.1 Getting started with gawk

Gawk is the GNU version of the commonly available UNIX **awk** program, another popular stream editor. Since the **awk** program is often just a link to **gawk**, we will refer to it as **awk**.

The basic function of **awk** is to search files for lines or other text units containing one or more patterns. When a line matches one of the patterns, special actions are performed on that line.

Programs in **awk** are different from programs in most other languages, because **awk** programs are "data-driven": you describe the data you want to work with and then what to do when you find it. Most other languages are "procedural." You have to describe, in great detail, every step the program is to take. When working with procedural languages, it is usually much harder to clearly describe the data your program will process. For this reason, **awk** programs are often refreshingly easy to read and write.

6.1.1 Gawk commands

When you run **awk**, you specify an **awk** *program* that tells **awk** what to do. The program consists of a series of *rules*. (It may also contain function definitions, loops, conditions and other programming constructs, advanced features that we will ignore for now.) Each rule specifies one pattern to search for and one action to perform upon finding the pattern.

There are several ways to run **awk**. If the program is short, it is easiest to run it on the command line:

```
awk PROGRAM inputfile(s)
```

If multiple changes have to be made, possibly regularly and on multiple files, it is easier to put the **awk** commands in a script. This is read like this:

```
awk -f PROGRAM-FILE inputfile(s)
```

6.2 The print program

The **print** command in **awk** outputs selected data from the input file.

When **awk** reads a line of a file, it divides the line in fields based on the specified *input field separator*, FS, which is an **awk** variable (see Section 6.3.2). This variable is predefined to be one or more spaces or tabs.

The variables $1, $2, $3, ..., $N hold the values of the first, second, third until the last field of an input line. The variable $0 (zero) holds the value of the entire line. This is depicted in the image below, where we see six colums in the output of the **df** command:

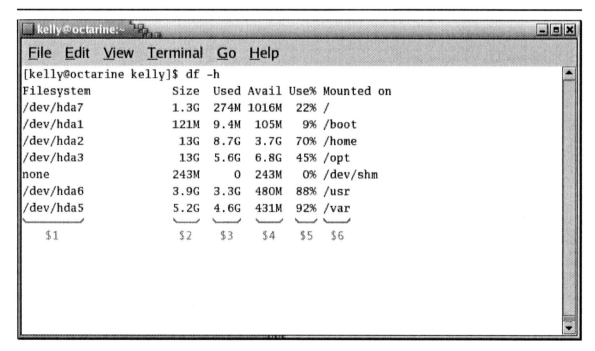

Figure 6.1: Fields in awk

In the output of **ls -1**, there are 9 columns. The **print** statement uses these fields as follows:

```
kelly@octarine ~/test> ls -l | awk '{ print $9 $5 }'
160orig
121script.sed
120temp_file
126test
120twolines
441txt2html.sh

kelly@octarine ~/test>
```

This command printed the fifth column of a long file listing, which contains the
file size, and the last column, the name of the file. This output is not very readable unless you use the official way of referring to columns, which is to separate
the ones that you want to print with a comma. In that case, the default output
separater character, usually a space, will be put in between each output field.

6.2.1 Formatting fields

Without formatting, using only the output separator, the output looks rather poor.
Inserting a couple of tabs and a string to indicate what output this is will make it
look a lot better:

```
kelly@octarine ~/test> ls -ldh * | grep -v total | \
awk '{ print "Size is " $5 " bytes for " $9 }'
Size is 160 bytes for orig
Size is 121 bytes for script.sed
Size is 120 bytes for temp_file
Size is 126 bytes for test
Size is 120 bytes for twolines
Size is 441 bytes for txt2html.sh

kelly@octarine ~/test>
```

Note the use of the backslash, which makes long input continue on the next line
without the shell interpreting this as a separate command. While your command
line input can be of virtually unlimited length, your monitor is not, and printed
paper certainly isn't. Using the backslash also allows for copying and pasting of
the above lines into a terminal window.

The -h option to **ls** is used for supplying humanly readable size formats for bigger
files. The output of a long listing displaying the total amount of blocks in the
directory is given when a directory is the argument. This line is useless to us, so
we add an asterisk. We also add the -d option for the same reason, in case asterisk
expands to a directory.

The backslash in this example marks the continuation of a line. See Section 3.3.2.

You can take out any number of columns and even reverse the order. In the example below this is demonstrated for showing the most critical partitions:

```
kelly@octarine ~> df -h | sort -rnk 5 | head -3 | \
awk '{ print "Partition " $6 "\t: " $5 " full!" }'
Partition /var  : 86% full!
Partition /usr  : 85% full!
Partition /home : 70% full!

kelly@octarine ~>
```

Table 6.1 gives an overview of special formatting characters:

Table 6.1: Formatting characters for gawk

Sequence	Meaning
\a	Bell character
\n	Newline character
\t	Tab

Quotes, dollar signs and other meta-characters should be escaped with a backslash.

6.2.2   The print command and regular expressions

A regular expression can be used as a pattern by enclosing it in slashes. The regular expression is then tested against the entire text of each record. The syntax is as follows:

```
awk 'EXPRESSION { PROGRAM }' file(s)
```

The following example displays only local disk device information, networked file systems are not shown:

```
kelly is in ~> df -h | awk '/dev\/hd/ { print $6 "\t: " $5 }'
/        : 46%
/boot    : 10%
/opt     : 84%
/usr     : 97%
/var     : 73%
/.vol1   : 8%

kelly is in ~>
```

Slashes need to be escaped, because they have a special meaning to the **awk** program.

Below another example where we search the /etc directory for files ending in ".conf" and starting with either "a" or "x":

```
kelly is in /etc> ls -l | awk '/\<[a|x].*\.conf$/ { print $9 }'
amd.conf
antivir.conf
xcdroast.conf
xinetd.conf

kelly is in /etc>
```

This example illustrates the special meaning of the dot in regular expressions: the first one indicates that we want to search for any character after the first search string, the second is escaped because it is part of a string to find (the end of the file name).

6.2.3 Special patterns

In order to precede output with comments, use the **BEGIN** statement:

```
kelly is in /etc> ls -l | \
awk 'BEGIN { print "Files found:\n" } /\<[a|x].*\.conf$/ { print $9 }'
Files found:
amd.conf
antivir.conf
xcdroast.conf
xinetd.conf

kelly is in /etc>
```

The **END** statement can be added for inserting text after the entire input is processed:

```
kelly is in /etc> ls -l | \
awk '/\<[a|x].*\.conf$/ { print $9 } END { print \
"Can I do anything else for you, mistress?" }'
amd.conf
antivir.conf
xcdroast.conf
xinetd.conf
Can I do anything else for you, mistress?

kelly is in /etc>
```

6.2.4 Gawk scripts

As commands tend to get a little longer, you might want to put them in a script, so they are reusable. An **awk** script contains **awk** statements defining patterns and actions.

As an illustration, we will build a report that displays our most loaded partitions. See Section 6.2.1.

```
kelly is in ~> cat diskrep.awk
BEGIN { print "*** WARNING WARNING WARNING ***" }
/\<[8|9][0-9]%/ { print "Partition " $6 "\t: " $5 " full!" }
END { print "*** Give money for new disks URGENTLY! ***" }

kelly is in ~> df -h | awk -f diskrep.awk
*** WARNING WARNING WARNING ***
Partition /usr  : 97% full!
*** Give money for new disks URGENTLY! ***

kelly is in ~>
```

awk first prints a begin message, then formats all the lines that contain an eight or a nine at the beginning of a word, followed by one other number and a percentage sign. An end message is added.

 Syntax highlighting

Awk is a programming language. Its syntax is recognized by most editors that can do syntax highlighting for other languages, such as C, Bash, HTML, etc.

6.3 Gawk variables

As **awk** is processing the input file, it uses several variables. Some are editable, some are read-only.

6.3.1 The input field separator

The *field separator*, which is either a single character or a regular expression, controls the way **awk** splits up an input record into fields. The input record is scanned for character sequences that match the separator definition; the fields themselves are the text between the matches.

The field separator is represented by the built-in variable FS. Note that this is something different from the IFS variable used by POSIX-compliant shells.

The value of the field separator variable can be changed in the **awk** program with the assignment operator =. Often the right time to do this is at the beginning of execution before any input has been processed, so that the very first record is read with the proper separator. To do this, use the special **BEGIN** pattern.

In the example below, we build a command that displays all the users on your system with a description:

```
kelly is in ~> awk 'BEGIN { FS=":" } { print $1 "\t" $5 }' /etc/passwd
--output omitted--
kelly     Kelly Smith
franky    Franky B.
eddy      Eddy White
willy     William Black
cathy     Catherine the Great
sandy     Sandy Li Wong

kelly is in ~>
```

In an **awk** script, it would look like this:

```
kelly is in ~> cat printnames.awk
BEGIN { FS=":" }
{ print $1 "\t" $5 }

kelly is in ~> awk -f printnames.awk /etc/passwd
--output omitted--
```

Choose input field separators carefully to prevent problems. An example to illustrate this: say you get input in the form of lines that look like this:

"Sandy L. Wong, 64 Zoo St., Antwerp, 2000X"

You write a command line or a script, which prints out the name of the person in that record:

```
awk 'BEGIN { FS="," } { print $1, $2, $3 }' inputfile
```

But a person might have a PhD, and it might be written like this:

"Sandy L. Wong, PhD, 64 Zoo St., Antwerp, 2000X"

Your **awk** will give the wrong output for this line. If needed, use an extra **awk** or **sed** to uniform data input formats.

The default input field separator is one or more whitespaces or tabs.

6.3.2   The output field separator

Fields are normally separated by spaces in the output. This becomes apparent when you use the correct syntax for the **print** command, where arguments are separated by commas:

```
kelly@octarine ~/test> cat test
record1          data1
record2          data2

kelly@octarine ~/test> awk '{ print $1 $2}' test
record1data1
record2data2

kelly@octarine ~/test> awk '{ print $1, $2}' test
record1 data1
record2 data2

kelly@octarine ~/test>
```

If you don't put in the commas, **print** will treat the items to output as one argument, thus omitting the use of the default *output separator*, OFS.

Any character string may be used as the output field separator by setting this built-in variable.

6.3.3   The output record separator

The output from an entire **print** statement is called an *output record*. Each **print** command results in one output record, and then outputs a string called the *output record separator*, ORS. The default value for this variable is "\n", a newline character. Thus, each **print** statement generates a separate line.

To change the way output fields and records are separated, assign new values to OFS and ORS:

```
kelly@octarine ~/test> awk 'BEGIN { OFS=";" ; ORS="\n-->\n" } \
{ print $1,$2}' test
record1;data1
-->
record2;data2
-->

kelly@octarine ~/test>
```

If the value of ORS does not contain a newline, the program's output is run together on a single line.

6.3.4   The number of records

The built-in NR holds the number of records that are processed. It is incremented after reading a new input line. You can use it at the end to count the total number of records, or in each output record:

```
kelly@octarine ~/test> cat processed.awk
BEGIN { OFS="-" ; ORS="\n--> done\n" }
{ print "Record number " NR ":\t" $1,$2 }
END { print "Number of records processed: " NR }

kelly@octarine ~/test> awk -f processed.awk test
Record number 1:         record1-data1
--> done
Record number 2:         record2-data2
--> done
Number of records processed: 2
--> done

kelly@octarine ~/test>
```

6.3.5   User defined variables

Apart from the built-in variables, you can define your own. When **awk** encounters a reference to a variable which does not exist (which is not predefined), the variable is created and initialized to a null string. For all subsequent references, the value of the variable is whatever value was assigned last. Variables can be a string or a numeric value. Content of input fields can also be assigned to variables.

Values can be assigned directly using the = operator, or you can use the current value of the variable in combination with other operators:

```
kelly@octarine ~> cat revenues
20021009        20021013        consultancy    BigComp        2500
20021015        20021020        training       EduComp        2000
20021112        20021123        appdev         SmartComp      10000
20021204        20021215        training       EduComp        5000

kelly@octarine ~> cat total.awk
{ total=total + $5 }
{ print "Send bill for " $5 " dollar to " $4 }
END { print "-------------------------------\nTotal revenue: " total }

kelly@octarine ~> awk -f total.awk test
Send bill for 2500 dollar to BigComp
Send bill for 2000 dollar to EduComp
Send bill for 10000 dollar to SmartComp
Send bill for 5000 dollar to EduComp
-------------------------------
Total revenue: 19500

kelly@octarine ~>
```

C-like shorthands like **VAR+= value** are also accepted.

6.3.6   More examples

The example from Section 5.3.2 becomes much easier when we use an **awk** script:

```
kelly@octarine ~/html> cat make-html-from-text.awk
BEGIN { print "<html>\n<head><title>Awk-generated HTML</title></head>\n<body \
bgcolor=\"#ffffff\">\n<pre>" }
{ print $0 }
END { print "</pre>\n</body>\n</html<" }
```

And the command to execute is also much more straightforward when using **awk** instead of **sed**:

```
kelly@octarine ~/html> awk -f make-html-from-text.awk testfile > file.html
```

 Awk examples on your system

> We refer again to the directory containing the initscripts on your system. Enter a command similar to the following to see more practical examples of the widely spread usage of the **awk** command:

> `grep awk /etc/init.d/*`

6.3.7 The printf program

For more precise control over the output format than what is normally provided by **print**, use **printf**. The **printf** command can be used to specify the field width to use for each item, as well as various formatting choices for numbers (such as what output base to use, whether to print an exponent, whether to print a sign, and how many digits to print after the decimal point). This is done by supplying a string, called the *format string*, that controls how and where to print the other arguments.

The syntax is the same as for the C-language **printf** statement; see your C introduction guide. The **gawk** info pages contain full explanations.

6.4 Summary

The **gawk** utility interprets a special-purpose programming language, handling simple data-reformatting jobs with just a few lines of code. It is the free version of the general UNIX **awk** command.

This tools reads lines of input data and can easily recognize columned output. The **print** program is the most common for filtering and formatting defined fields.

On-the-fly variable declaration is straightforward and allows for simple calculation of sums, statistics and other operations on the processed input stream. Variables and commands can be put in **awk** scripts for background processing.

6.5 Exercises

These are some practical examples where **awk** can be useful.

1. For the first exercise, your input is lines in the following form:

```
Username:Firstname:Lastname:Telephone number
```

   Make an **awk** script that will convert such a line to an LDAP record in this format:

```
dn: uid=Username, dc=example, dc=com
cn: Firstname Lastname
sn: Lastname
telephoneNumber: Telephone number
```

   Create a file containing a couple of test records and check.

2. Create a Bash script using **awk** and standard UNIX commands that will show the top three users of disk space in the /home file system (if you don't have the directory holding the homes on a separate partition, make the script for the / partition; this is present on every UNIX system). First, execute the commands from the command line. Then put them in a script. The script should create sensible output (sensible as in readable by the boss). If everything proves to work, have the script email its results to you (use for instance **mail -s Disk space usage you@your_comp result**).

   If the quota daemon is running, use that information; if not, use **find**.

3. Create XML-style output from a **Tab**-separated list in the following form:

```
Meaning very long line with a lot of description

meaning another long line

othermeaning    more longline

testmeaning     loooooooooooooong line, but i mean really loooooooooooooong.
```

The output should read:

```
<row>
<entry>Meaning</entry>
<entry>
very long line
</entry>
</row>
<row>
<entry>meaning</entry>
<entry>
long line
</entry>
</row>
<row>
<entryothermeaning</entry>
<entry>
more longline
</entry>
</row>
<row>
<entrytestmeaning</entry>
<entry>
loooooooooooooooooooooong line, but i mean really loooooooooooooooooooooong.
</entry>
</row>
```

Additionally, if you know anything about XML, write a BEGIN and END script to complete the table. Or do it in HTML.

Chapter 7

Conditional statements

In this chapter we will discuss the use of conditionals in Bash scripts. This includes the following topics:

- *The **if** statement*
- *Using the exit status of a command*
- *Comparing and testing input and files*
- ***if/then/else** constructs*
- ***if/then/elif/else** constructs*
- *Using and testing the positional parameters*
- *Nested **if** statements*
- *Boolean expressions*
- *Using **case** statements*

7.1 Introduction to if

At times you need to specify different courses of action to be taken in a shell script, depending on the success or failure of a command. The **if** construction allows you to specify such conditions.

The most compact syntax of the **if** command is:

```
if TEST-COMMANDS; then CONSEQUENT-COMMANDS; fi
```

The **TEST-COMMAND** list is executed, and if its return status is zero, the **CONSEQUENT-COMMANDS** list is executed. The return status is the exit status of the last command executed, or zero if no condition tested true.

The **TEST-COMMAND** often involves numerical or string comparison tests, but it can also be any command that returns a status of zero when it succeeds and some other status when it fails. Unary expressions are often used to examine the status of a file. If the FILE argument to one of the primaries is of the form /dev/fd/N, then file descriptor "N" is checked. stdin, stdout and stderr and their respective file descriptors may also be used for tests.

Expressions used with if

The table below contains an overview of the so-called "primaries" that make up the **TEST-COMMAND** command or list of commands. These primaries are put between square brackets to indicate the test of a conditional expression.

Table 7.1: Primary expressions

Primary	Meaning
[-aFILE]	True if FILE exists.
[-bFILE]	True if FILE exists and is a block-special file.
[-cFILE]	True if FILE exists and is a character-special file.
[-dFILE]	True if FILE exists and is a directory.
[-eFILE]	True if FILE exists.
[-fFILE]	True if FILE exists and is a regular file.
[-gFILE]	True if FILE exists and its SGID bit is set.
[-hFILE]	True if FILE exists and is a symbolic link.
[-kFILE]	True if FILE exists and its sticky bit is set.
[-pFILE]	True if FILE exists and is a named pipe (FIFO).
[-rFILE]	True if FILE exists and is readable.
[-sFILE]	True if FILE exists and has a size greater than zero.
[-tFD]	True if file descriptor FD is open and refers to a terminal.
[-uFILE]	True if FILE exists and its SUID (set user ID) bit is set.
[-wFILE]	True if FILE True if FILE exists and is writable.

[-xFILE]	True if FILE exists and is executable.
[-OFILE]	True if FILE exists and is owned by the effective user ID.
[-GFILE]	True if FILE exists and is owned by the effective group ID.
[-LFILE]	True if FILE exists and is a symbolic link.
[-NFILE]	True if FILE exists and has been modified since it was last read.
[-SFILE]	True if FILE exists and is a socket.
[FILE1-ntFILE2]	True if FILE1 has been changed more recently than FILE2, or if FILE1 exists and FILE2 does not.
[FILE1-otFILE2]	True if FILE1 is older than FILE2, or is FILE2 exists and FILE1 does not.
[FILE1-efFILE2]	True if FILE1 and FILE2 refer to the same device and inode numbers.
[-o OPTIONNAME]	True if shell option "OPTIONNAME" is enabled.
[-z STRING]	True of the length of "STRING" is zero.
[-n STRING] or [STRING]	True of the length of "STRING" is non-zero.
[STRING1 == STRING2]	True if the strings are equal. "=" may be used instead of "==" for strict POSIX compliance.
[STRING1 != STRING2]	True if the strings are not equal.
[STRING1 < STRING2]	True if "STRING1" sorts before "STRING2" lexicographically in the current locale.
[STRING1 > STRING2]	True if "STRING1" sorts after "STRING2" lexicographically in the current locale.
[ARG1 OP ARG2]	"OP" is one of -eq, -ne, -lt, -le, -gt or -ge. These arithmetic binary operators return true if "ARG1" is equal to, not equal to, less than, less than or equal to, greater than, or greater than or equal to "ARG2", respectively. "ARG1" and "ARG2" are integers.

Expressions may be combined using the operators in Table 7.2, which are listed in decreasing order of precedence.

Table 7.2: Combining expressions

Operation	Effect
[! EXPR]	True if **EXPR** is false.
[(EXPR)]	Returns the value of **EXPR**. This may be used to override the normal precedence of operators.
[EXPR1 -a EXPR2]	True if both **EXPR1** and **EXPR2** are true.
[EXPR1 -o EXPR2]	True if either **EXPR1** or **EXPR2** is true.

The **[** (or **test**) built-in evaluates conditional expressions using a set of rules based on the number of arguments. More information about this subject can be found in the Bash documentation. Just like the **if** is closed with **fi**, the opening angular bracket should be closed after the conditions have been listed.

Commands following the then statement

The **CONSEQUENT-COMMANDS** list that follows the **then** statement can be any valid UNIX command, any executable program, any executable shell script or any shell statement, with the exception of the closing **fi**. It is important to remember that the **then** and **fi** are considered to be separated statements in the shell. Therefore, when issued on the command line, they are separated by a semi-colon.

In a script, the different parts of the **if** statement are usually well-separated. Below, a couple of simple examples.

Checking files

The first example checks for the existence of a file:

```
anny ~> cat msgcheck.sh
#!/bin/bash

echo "This scripts checks the existence of the messages file."
echo "Checking..."
if [ -f /var/log/messages ]
  then
    echo "/var/log/messages exists."
fi
echo
echo "...done."

anny ~> ./msgcheck.sh
This scripts checks the existence of the messages file.
Checking...
/var/log/messages exists.

...done.
```

Checking shell options

To add in your Bash configuration files:

```
# These lines will print a message if the noclobber option is set:

if [ -o noclobber ]
  then
    echo "Your files are protected against accidental overwriting using redirection."
fi
```

The environment

The above example will work when entered on the command line:

```
anny ~> if [ -o noclobber ] ; then echo ; \
echo "your files are protected against overwriting." ; echo ; fi

your files are protected against overwriting.

anny ~>
```

However, if you use testing of conditions that depend on the environment, you might get different results when you enter the same command in a script, because the script will open a new shell, in which expected variables and options might not be set automatically.

7.1.1 Simple applications of if

In this section, we explore several useful things you can do with the **if** command.

Testing exit status

The ? variable holds the exit status of the previously executed command (the most recently completed foreground process).

The following example shows a simple test:

```
anny ~> if [ $? -eq 0 ]
More input> then echo 'That was a good job!'
More input> fi
That was a good job!

anny ~>
```

The following example demonstrates that **TEST-COMMANDS** might be any UNIX command that returns an exit status, and that **if** again returns an exit status of zero:

```
anny ~> if ! grep $USER /etc/passwd
More input> then echo "your user account is not managed locally"; fi
your user account is not managed locally

anny > echo $?
0

anny >
```

The same result can be obtained as follows:

```
anny > grep $USER /etc/passwd

anny > if [ $? -ne 0 ] ; then echo "not a local account" ; fi
not a local account

anny >
```

Numeric comparisons

The examples below use numerical comparisons:

```
anny > num=`wc -l work.txt`

anny > echo $num
201

anny > if [ "num" > 150 ]
More input> then echo ; echo "you've worked hard enough for today."
More input> echo ; fi

you've worked hard enough for today.


anny >
```

This script is executed by cron every Sunday. If the week number is even, it reminds you to put out the garbage cans:

```
#!/bin/bash

# Calculate the week number using the date command:

WEEKOFFSET=$[ $(date +"%V") % 2 ]

# Test if we have a remainder.  If not, this is an even week so send
# a message. Else, do nothing.

if [ $WEEKOFFSET -eq "0" ]; then
  echo "Sunday evening, put out the garbage cans." | \
                        mail -s "Garbage cans out" your@your_domain.org
```

String comparisons

An example of comparing strings for testing the user ID:

```
if [ "$(whoami)" != 'root' ]; then
        echo "You have no permission to run $0 as non-root user."
        exit 1;
fi
```

With Bash, you can shorten this type of construct. The compact equivalent of the above test is as follows:

```
[ "$(whoami)" != 'root' ] && echo you are using a non-privileged account
```

Regular expressions may also be used:

```
anny > gender="female"

anny > if [[ "$gender" == "f*" ]]
More input> then echo "Pleasure to meet you, Madame."; fi
Pleasure to meet you, Madame.

anny >
```

See the info pages for Bash for more information on pattern matching with the "((EXPRESSION))" and "[[EXPRESSION]]" constructs.

7.2 if/then/else constructs

Dummy example

This is the construct to use to take one course of action if the **if** commands test true, and another if it tests false. An example:

```
freddy scripts> gender="male"

freddy scripts> if [[ "$gender" == "f*" ]]
More input> then echo "Pleasure to meet you, Madame."
More input> else echo "How come the lady hasn't got a drink yet?"
More input> fi
How come the lady hasn't got a drink yet?

freddy scripts>
```

Like the **CONSEQUENT-COMMANDS** list following the **then** statement, the **ALTERNATE-CONSEQUENT-COMMANDS** list following the **else** statement can hold any UNIX-style command that returns an exit status.

Another example, extending the one from Section 7.1.1:

```
anny ~> su -
Password:
[root@elegance root]# if ! grep ^$USER /etc/passwd 1>/dev/null
> then echo "your user account is not managed locally"
> else echo "your account is managed from the local /etc/passwd file"
> fi
your account is managed from the local /etc/passwd file
[root@elegance root]#
```

We switch to the *root* account to demonstrate the effect of the **else** statement - your *root* is usually a local account while your own user account might be managed by a central system, such as an LDAP server.

Checking command line arguments

Instead of setting a variable and then executing a script, it is frequently more elegant to put the values for the variables on the command line.

We use the positional parameters $1, $2, ..., $N for this purpose. $# refers to the number of command line arguments. $0 refers to the name of the script.

The following is a simple example:

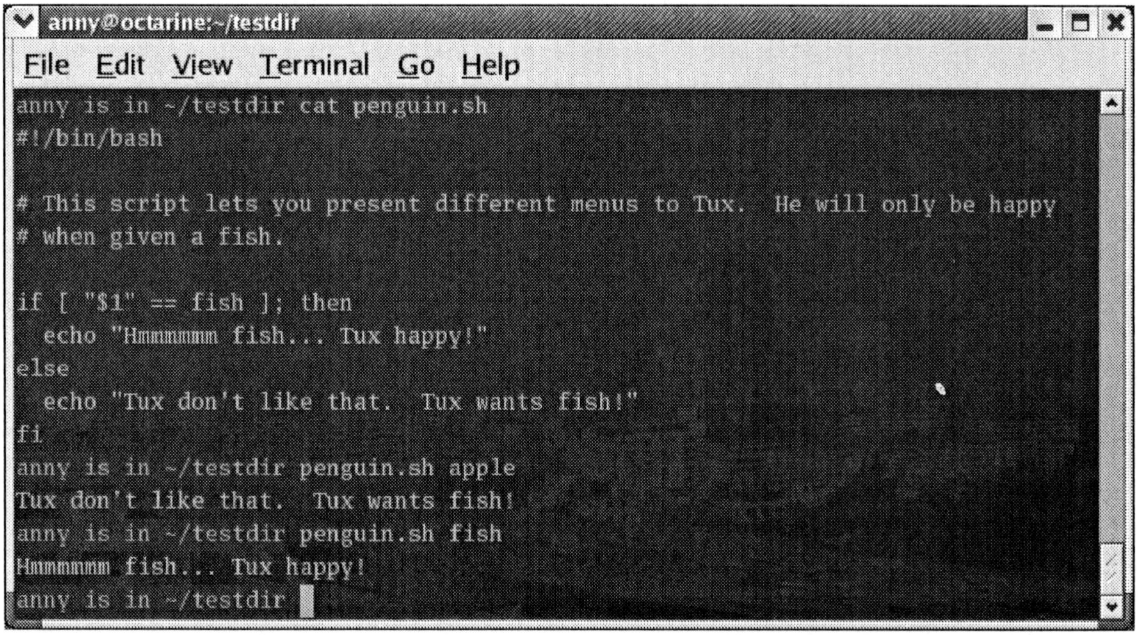
anny@octarine:~/testdir
File Edit View Terminal Go Help
anny is in ~/testdir cat penguin.sh
#!/bin/bash
# This script lets you present different menus to Tux. He will only be happy
# when given a fish.
if ["$1" == fish]; then
echo "Hmmmmmm fish... Tux happy!"
else
echo "Tux don't like that. Tux wants fish!"
fi
anny is in ~/testdir penguin.sh apple
Tux don't like that. Tux wants fish!
anny is in ~/testdir penguin.sh fish
Hmmmmmm fish... Tux happy!
anny is in ~/testdir

Figure 7.1: Testing of a command line argument with if

Here's another example, using two arguments:

```
anny ~> cat weight.sh
#!/bin/bash

# This script prints a message about your weight if you give it your
# weight in kilos and hight in centimeters.
weight="$1"
height="$2"
idealweight=$[$height - 110]
if [ $weight -le $idealweight ] ; then
  echo "You should eat a bit more fat."
else
  echo "You should eat a bit more fruit."
fi

anny ~> bash -x weight.sh 55 169
+ weight=55
+ height=169
+ idealweight=59
+ '[' 55 -le 59 ']'
+ echo 'You should eat a bit more fat.'
You should eat a bit more fat.
```

Testing the number of arguments

The following example shows how to change the previous script so that it prints a message if more or less than 2 arguments are given:

```
anny ~> cat weight.sh
#!/bin/bash

# This script prints a message about your weight if you give it your
# weight in kilos and hight in centimeters.

if [ ! $# == 2 ]; then
  echo "Usage: $0 weight_in_kilos length_in_centimeters"
  exit
fi

weight="$1"
height="$2"
idealweight=$[$height - 110]

if [ $weight -le $idealweight ] ; then
  echo "You should eat a bit more fat."
else
  echo "You should eat a bit more fruit."
fi

anny ~> weight sh 70 150
You should eat a bit more fruit.

anny ~> weight sh 70 150 33
Usage: ./weight.sh weight_in_kilos length_in_centimeters
```

The first argument is referred to as $1, the second as $2 and so on. The total number of arguments is stored in $#.

Check out Section 7.6 for a more elegant way to print usage messages.

Testing that a file exists

This test is done in a lot of scripts, because there's no use in starting a lot of programs if you know they're not going to work:

```
#!/bin/bash

# This script gives information about a file.

FILENAME="$1"

echo "Properties for $FILENAME:"
```

```
if [ -f $FILENAME ]; then
  echo "Size is $(ls -lh $FILENAME | awk '{ print $5 }')"
  echo "Type is $(file $FILENAME | cut -d":" -f2 -)"
  echo "Inode number is $(ls -i $FILENAME | cut -d" " -f1 -)"
  echo "$(df -h $FILENAME | grep -v Mounted | awk '{ print "On",$1", \
which is mounted as the",$6,"partition."}')"
else
  echo "File does not exist."
fi
```

Note that the file is referred to using a variable; in this case it is the first argument to the script. Alternatively, when no arguments are given, file locations are usually stored in variables at the beginning of a script, and their content is referred to using these variables. Thus, when you want to change a file name in a script, you only need to do it once.

7.3 if/then/elif/else constructs

This is the full form of the **if** statement:

```
if TEST-COMMANDS; then

CONSEQUENT-COMMANDS;

elif MORE-TEST-COMMANDS; then

MORE-CONSEQUENT-COMMANDS;

else ALTERNATE-CONSEQUENT-COMMANDS; then

fi
```

The **TEST-COMMANDS** list is executed, and if its return status is zero, the **CONSEQUENT-COMMANDS** list is executed. If **TEST-COMMANDS** returns a non-zero status, each **elif** list is executed in turn, and if its exit status is zero, the corresponding **MORE-CONSEQUENT-COMMANDS** is executed and the command completes. If **else** is followed by an **ALTERNATE-CONSEQUENT-COMMANDS** list, and the final command in the final **if** or **elif** clause has a non-zero exit status, then **ALTERNATE-CONSEQUENT-COMMANDS** is executed. The return status is the exit status of the last command executed, or zero if no condition tested true.

7.3.1 Example

Here is an example that you can put in your crontab for daily execution:

```
anny /etc/cron.daily> cat disktest.sh
#!/bin/bash

# This script does a very simple test for checking disk space.

space=`df -h | awk '{print $5}' | grep % | grep -v Use | sort -n | tail -1 \
| cut -d "%" -f1 -`
alertvalue="80"

if [ "$space" -ge "$alertvalue" ]; then
  echo "At least one of my disks is nearly full!" | mail -s "daily
                                          diskcheck" root
else
  echo "Disk space normal" | mail -s "daily diskcheck" root
fi
```

7.4 Nested if statements

Inside the **if** statement, you can use another **if** statement. You may use as many levels of nested **if**s as you can logically manage.

This is an example testing leap years:

```
anny ~/testdir> cat testleap.sh
#!/bin/bash
# This script will test if we're in a leap year or not.

year=`date +%Y`

if [ $[$year % 400] -eq "0" ]; then
  echo "This is a leap year.  February has 29 days."
elif [ $[$year % 4] -eq 0 ]; then
        if [ $[$year % 100] -ne 0 ]; then
           echo "This is a leap year, February has 29 days."
        else
           echo "This is not a leap year.  February has 28 days."
        fi
else
  echo "This is not a leap year.  February has 28 days."
fi

anny ~/testdir> date
Tue Jan 14 20:37:55 CET 2003

anny ~/testdir> testleap.sh
This is not a leap year.
```

7.5 Boolean operations

The above script can be shortened using the Boolean operators "AND" (&&) and "OR" (||).

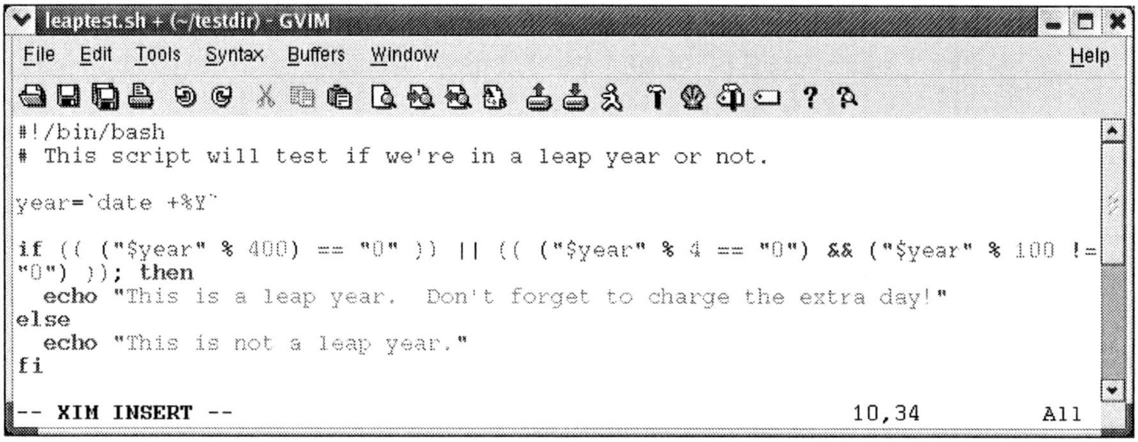
leaptest.sh + (~/testdir) - GVIM
File Edit Tools Syntax Buffers Window Help
#!/bin/bash
# This script will test if we're in a leap year or not.
year=`date +%Y`
if ((("$year" % 400) == "0")) || ((("$year" % 4 == "0") && ("$year" % 100 !=
"0"))); then
echo "This is a leap year. Don't forget to charge the extra day!"
else
echo "This is not a leap year."
fi
-- XIM INSERT --
10,34
All

Figure 7.2: Example using Boolean operators

We use the double brackets for testing an arithmetic expression; see Section 3.4.5. This is equivalent to the **let** statement. You will get stuck using angular brackets here, if you try something like **$[$year % 400]**, because here, the angular brackets don't represent an actual command by themselves.

Among other editors, **gvim** is one of those supporting colour schemes according to the file format; such editors are useful for detecting errors in your code.

7.6 Using the exit statement and if

We already briefly met the **exit** statement in Section 7.2. It terminates execution of the entire script. It is most often used if the input requested from the user is incorrect, if a statement did not run successfully or if some other error occurred.

The **exit** statement takes an optional argument. This argument is the integer exit status code, which is passed back to the parent and stored in the $? variable.

A zero argument means that the script ran successfully. Any other value may be used by programmers to pass back different messages to the parent, so that different actions can be taken according to failure or success of the child process. If no argument is given to the **exit** command, the parent shell uses the current value of the $? variable.

Below is an example with a slightly adapted penguin.sh script, which sends its exit status back to the parent, feed.sh:

```
anny ~/testdir> cat penguin.sh
#!/bin/bash

# This script lets you present different menus to Tux.  He will only be
# happy when given a fish.  We've also added a dolphin and (presumably)
# a camel.

if [ "$menu" == "fish" ]; then
  if [ "$animal" == "penguin" ]; then
    echo "Hmmmmmm fish... Tux happy!"
  elif [ "$animal" == "dolphin" ]; then
    echo "Pweetpeettreetppeterdepweet!"
  else
    echo "*prrrrrrrt*"
  fi
else
  if [ "$animal" == "penguin" ]; then
    echo "Tux don't like that.  Tux wants fish!"
    exit 1
  elif [ "$animal" == "dolphin" ]; then
    echo "Pweepwishpeeterdepweet!"
    exit 2
  else
    echo "Will you read this sign?!"
    exit 3
  fi
fi
```

This script is called upon in the next one, which therefore exports its variables menu and animal:

```
anny ~/testdir> cat feed.sh
#!/bin/bash
# This script acts upon the exit status given by penguin.sh

export menu="$1"
export animal="$2"

feed="/nethome/anny/testdir/penguin.sh"

$feed $menu $animal

case $? in

1)
  echo "Guard: You'd better give'm a fish, less they get violent..."
  ;;
2)
  echo "Guard: It's because of people like you that they are leaving earth \
all the time..."
  ;;
3)
  echo "Guard: Buy the food that the Zoo provides for the animals, you ***, \
how do you think we survive?"
  ;;
*)
  echo "Guard: Don't forget the guide!"
  ;;
esac

anny ~/testdir> ./feed.sh apple penguin
Tux don't like that.  Tux wants fish!
Guard: You'd better give'm a fish, less they get violent...
```

As you can see, exit status codes can be chosen freely. Existing commands usually have a series of defined codes; see the programmer's manual for each command for more information.

7.7 Using case statements

Nested **if** statements might be nice, but as soon as you are confronted with a couple of different possible actions to take, they tend to confuse. For the more complex conditionals, use the **case** syntax:

```
case EXPRESSION in CASE1) COMMAND-LIST;; CASE2) COMMAND-
LIST;; ... CASEN) COMMAND-LIST;; esac
```

Each case is an expression matching a pattern. The commands in the **COMMAND-LIST** for the first match are executed. The "|" symbol is used for separating multiple patterns, and the ")" operator terminates a pattern list. Each case plus its according commands are called a *clause*. Each clause must be terminated with ";;". Each **case** statement is ended with the **esac** statement.

In the example, we demonstrate use of cases for sending a more selective warning message with the `disktest.sh` script:

```
anny ~/testdir> cat disktest.sh
#!/bin/bash

# This script does a very simple test for checking disk space.

space=`df -h | awk '{print $5}' | grep % | grep -v Use | sort -n | tail -1 \
| cut -d "%" -f1 -`

case $space in
[1-6]*)
  Message="All is quiet."
  ;;
[7-8]*)
  Message="Start thinking about cleaning out some stuff.  There's a partition \
that is $space % full."
  ;;
9[1-8])
  Message="Better hurry with that new disk...  One partition is $space % full."
  ;;
99)
  Message="I'm drowning here!  There's a partition at $space %!"
  ;;
*)
  Message="I seem to be running with an nonexitent amount of disk space..."
  ;;
esac

echo $Message | mail -s "disk report `date`" anny
```

```
anny ~/testdir>
You have new mail.

anny ~/testdir> tail -16 /var/spool/mail/anny
From anny@octarine Tue Jan 14 22:10:47 2003
Return-Path: <anny@octarine>
Received: from octarine (localhost [127.0.0.1])
        by octarine (8.12.5/8.12.5) with ESMTP id h0ELAlBG020414
        for <anny@octarine>; Tue, 14 Jan 2003 22:10:47 +0100
Received: (from anny@localhost)
        by octarine (8.12.5/8.12.5/Submit) id h0ELAltn020413
        for anny; Tue, 14 Jan 2003 22:10:47 +0100
Date: Tue, 14 Jan 2003 22:10:47 +0100
From: Anny <anny@octarine>
Message-Id: <200301142110.h0ELAltn020413@octarine>
To: anny@octarine
Subject: disk report Tue Jan 14 22:10:47 CET 2003

Start thinking about cleaning out some stuff.  There's a partition that is 87 % \
full.

anny ~/testdir>
```

Of course you could have opened your mail program to check the results; this is just to demonstrate that the script sends a decent mail with "To:", "Subject:" and "From:" header lines.

Many more examples using **case** statements can be found in your system's init script directory. The startup scripts use **start** and **stop** cases to run or stop system processes. A theoretical example can be found in the next section.

7.7.1 Initscript example

Initscripts often make use of **case** statements for starting, stopping and querying system services. This is an excerpt of the script that starts Anacron, a daemon that runs commands periodically with a frequency specified in days.

```
case "$1" in
        start)
                start
                ;;

        stop)
                stop
                ;;

        status)
                status anacron
                ;;
        restart)
                stop
                start
                ;;
        condrestart)
                if test "x`pidof anacron`" != x; then
                        stop
                        start
                fi
                ;;

        *)
                echo $"Usage: $0 {start|stop|restart|condrestart|status}"
                exit 1

esac
```

The tasks to execute in each case, such as stopping and starting the daemon, are defined in functions, which are partially sourced from the /etc/rc.d/init.d/ functions file. See Chapter 11, "Functions" for more explanation.

7.8 Summary

In this chapter we learned how to build conditions into our scripts so that different actions can be undertaken upon success or failure of a command. The actions can be determined using the **if** statement. This allows you to perform arithmetic and string comparisons, and testing of exit code, input and files needed by the script.

A simple **if/then/fi** test often preceeds commands in a shell script in order to prevent output generation, so that the script can easily be run in the background or through the cron facility. More complex definitions of conditions are usually put in a **case** statement.

Upon successful condition testing, the script can explicitly inform the parent using the **exit 0** status. Upon failure, any other number may be returned. Based on the return code, the parent program can take appropriate action.

7.9 Exercises

Here are some ideas to get you started using **if** in scripts:

1. Use an **if/then/elif/else** construct that prints information about the current month. The script should print the number of days in this month, and give information about leap years if the current month is February.

2. Do the same, using a **case** statement and an alternative use of the **date** command.

3. Modify /etc/profile so that you get a special greeting message when you connect to your system as *root*.

4. Edit the leaptest.sh script from Section 7.5 so that it requires one argument, the year. Test that exactly one argument is supplied.

5. Write a script called whichdaemon.sh that checks if the **httpd** and **init** daemons are running on your system. If an **httpd** is running, the script should print a message like, "This machine is running a web server." Use **ps** to check on processes.

6. Write a script that makes a backup of your home directory on a remote machine using **scp**. The script should report in a log file, for instance ~/log/ homebackup.log. If you don't have a second machine to copy the backup to, use **scp** to test copying it to the localhost. This requires SSH keys between the two hosts, or else you have to supply a password. The creation of SSH keys is explained in **man *ssh-keygen***.

   The script should use **tar cf** for the creation of the backup and **gzip** or **bzip2** for compressing the .tar file. Put all filenames in variables. Put the name of the remote server and the remote directory in a variable. This will make it easier to re-use the script or to make changes to it in the future.

   The script should check for the existence of a compressed archive. If this exists, remove it first in order to prevent output generation.

   The script should also check for available diskspace. Keep in mind that at any given moment you could have the data in your home directory, the data in the .tar file and the data in the compressed archive all together on your disk. If there is not enough diskspace, exit with an error message in the log file.

   The script should clean up the compressed archive before it exits.

Chapter 8

Writing interactive scripts

In this chapter we will discuss how to interact with the users of our scripts:

- *Printing user friendly messages and explanations*
- *Catching user input*
- *Prompting for user input*
- *Using the file descriptors to read from and write to multiple files*

8.1 Displaying user messages

Some scripts run without any interaction from the user at all. Advantages of non-interactive scripts include:

- The script runs in a predictable way every time.
- The script can run in the background.

Many scripts, however, require input from the user, or give output to the user as the script is running. The advantages of interactive scripts are, among others:

- More flexible scripts can be built.
- Users can customize the script as it runs or make it behave in different ways.
- The script can report its progress as it runs.

When writing interactive scripts, never hold back on comments. A script that prints appropriate messages is much more user-friendly and can be more easily debugged. A script might do a perfect job, but you will get a whole lot of support calls if it does not inform the user about what it is doing. So include messages that tell the user to wait for output because a calculation is being done. If possible, try to give an indication of how long the user will have to wait. If the waiting should regularly take a long time when executing a certain task, you might want to consider integrating some processing indication in the output of your script.

When prompting the user for input, it is also better to give too much than too little information about the kind of data to be entered. This applies to the checking of arguments and the accompanying usage message as well.

Bash has the **echo** and **printf** commands to provide comments for users, and although you should be familiar with at least the use of **echo** by now, we will discuss some more examples in the next sections.

8.1.1 Using the echo built-in command

The **echo** built-in command outputs its arguments, separated by spaces and terminated with a newline character. The return status is always zero. **echo** takes a couple of options:

- -e: interprets backslash-escaped characters.
- -n: suppresses the trailing newline.

As an example of adding comments, we will make the `feed.sh` and `penguin.sh` from Section 7.2 a bit better:

```
michel ~/test> cat penguin.sh
#!/bin/bash

# This script lets you present different menus to Tux.  He will only be
# happy when given a fish.  To make it more fun, we added a couple more
# animals.

if [ "$menu" == "fish" ]; then
  if [ "$animal" == "penguin" ]; then
    echo -e "Hmmmmmm fish... Tux happy!\n"
  elif [ "$animal" == "dolphin" ]; then
    echo -e "\a\a\aPweetpeettreetppeterdepweet!\a\a\a\n"
  else
    echo -e "*prrrrrrrt*\n"
  fi
else
  if [ "$animal" == "penguin" ]; then
    echo -e "Tux don't like that.  Tux wants fish!\n"
    exit 1
  elif [ "$animal" == "dolphin" ]; then
    echo -e "\a\a\a\a\a\aPweepwishpeeterdepweet!\a\a\a"
    exit 2
  else
    echo -e "Will you read this sign?!  Don't feed the "$animal"s!\n"
    exit 3
  fi
fi

michel ~/test> cat feed.sh
#!/bin/bash
# This script acts upon the exit status given by penguin.sh

if [ "$#" != "2" ]; then
  echo -e "Usage of the feed script:\t$0 food-on-menu animal-name\n"
  exit 1
else

  export menu="$1"
  export animal="$2"

  echo -e "Feeding $menu to $animal...\n"

  feed="/nethome/anny/testdir/penguin.sh"

  $feed $menu $animal

result="$?"

  echo -e "Done feeding.\n"

case "$result" in
```

```
   1)
     echo -e "Guard: \"You'd better give'm a fish, less they get violent...\"\n"
     ;;
   2)
     echo -e "Guard: \"No wonder they flee our planet...\"\n"
     ;;
   3)
     echo -e "Guard: \"Buy the food that the Zoo provides at the entry, you ***\"\n"
     echo -e "Guard: \"You want to poison them, do you?\"\n"
     ;;
   *)
     echo -e "Guard: \"Don't forget the guide!\"\n"
     ;;
   esac

fi

echo "Leaving..."
echo -e "\a\a\aThanks for visiting the Zoo, hope to see you again soon!\n"

michel ~/test> feed.sh apple camel
Feeding apple to camel...

Will you read this sign?!  Don't feed the camels!

Done feeding.

Guard: "Buy the food that the Zoo provides at the entry, you ***"

Guard: "You want to poison them, do you?"

Leaving...
Thanks for visiting the Zoo, hope to see you again soon!

michel ~/test> feed.sh apple
Usage of the feed script:        ./feed.sh food-on-menu animal-name
```

More about escape characters can be found in Section 3.3.2. The following table gives an overview of sequences recognized by the **echo** command:

Table 8.1: Escape sequences used by the echo command

Sequence	Meaning
\a	Alert (bell).
\b	Backspace.
\c	Suppress trailing newline.
\e	Escape.
\f	Form feed.
\n	Newline.
\r	Carriage return.
\t	Horizontal tab.
\v	Vertical tab.

\\	Backslash.
\0NNN	The eight-bit character whose value is the octal value NNN (zero to three octal digits).
\NNN	The eight-bit character whose value is the octal value NNN (one to three octal digits).
\xHH	The eight-bit character whose value is the hexadecimal value (one or two hexadecimal digits).

For more information about the **printf** command and the way it allows you to format output; see the Bash info pages.

8.2 Catching user input

The **read** built-in command is the counterpart of the **echo** and **printf** commands. The syntax of the **read** command is as follows:

```
read [options] NAME1 NAME2 ...  NAMEN
```

One line is read from the standard input, or from the file descriptor supplied as an argument to the -u option. The first word of the line is assigned to the first name, NAME1, the second word to the second name, and so on, with leftover words and their intervening separators assigned to the last name, NAMEN. If there are fewer words read from the input stream than there are names, the remaining names are assigned empty values.

The characters in the value of the IFS variable are used to split the input line into words or tokens; see Section 3.4.7. The backslash character may be used to remove any special meaning for the next character read and for line continuation.

If no names are supplied, the line read is assigned to the variable REPLY.

The return code of the **read** command is zero, unless an end-of-file character is encountered, if **read** times out or if an invalid file descriptor is supplied as the argument to the -u option.

The following options are supported by the Bash **read** built-in:

Table 8.2: Options to the read built-in

Option	Meaning
-a ANAME	The words are assigned to sequential indexes of the array variable ANAME, starting at 0. All elements are removed from ANAME before the assignment. Other NAME arguments are ignored.

-d DELIM	The first character of DELIM is used to terminate the input line, rather than newline.
-e	**readline** is used to obtain the line.
-n NCHARS	**read** returns after reading NCHARS characters rather than waiting for a complete line of input.
-p PROMPT	Display PROMPT, without a trailing newline, before attempting to read any input. The prompt is displayed only if input is coming from a terminal.
-r	If this option is given, backslash does not act as an escape character. The backslash is considered to be part of the line. In particular, a backslash-newline pair may not be used as a line continuation.
-s	Silent mode. If input is coming from a terminal, characters are not echoed.
-t TIMEOUT	Cause **read** to time out and return failure if a complete line of input is not read within TIMEOUT seconds. This option has no effect if **read** is not reading input from the terminal or from a pipe.
-u FD	Read input from file descriptor FD.

This is a straightforward example, improving on the leaptest.sh script from the previous chapter:

```
michel ~/test> cat leaptest.sh
#!/bin/bash
# This script will test if you have given a leap year or not.

echo "Type the year that you want to check (4 digits), followed by [ENTER]:"

read year

if (( ("$year" % 400) == "0" )) || (( ("$year" % 4 == "0") && ("$year"
% 100 != "0") )); then
  echo "$year is a leap year."
else
  echo "This is not a leap year."
fi

michel ~/test> leaptest.sh
Type the year that you want to check (4 digits), followed by [ENTER]:
2000
2000 is a leap year.
```

8.2.1 Prompting for user input

The following example shows how you can use prompts to explain what the user should enter.

```
michel ~/test> cat friends.sh
#!/bin/bash

# This is a program that keeps your address book up to date.

friends="/var/tmp/michel/friends"

echo "Hello, "$USER".  This script will register you in Michel's friends database."

echo -n "Enter your name and press [ENTER]: "
read name
echo -n "Enter your gender and press [ENTER]: "
read -n 1 gender
echo

grep -i "$name" "$friends"

if  [ $? == 0 ]; then
  echo "You are already registered, quitting."
  exit 1
elif [ "$gender" == "m" ]; then
  echo "You are added to Michel's friends list."
  exit 1
else
  echo -n "How old are you? "
  read age
  if [ $age -lt 25 ]; then
    echo -n "Which colour of hair do you have? "
    read colour
    echo "$name $age $colour" >> "$friends"
    echo "You are added to Michel's friends list.  Thank you so much!"
  else
    echo "You are added to Michel's friends list."
    exit 1
  fi
fi

michel ~/test> cp friends.sh /var/tmp; cd /var/tmp

michel ~/test> touch friends; chmod a+w friends

michel ~/test> friends.sh
Hello, michel.  This script will register you in Michel's friends database.
Enter your name and press [ENTER]: michel
Enter your gender and press [ENTER] :m
You are added to Michel's friends list.

michel ~/test> cat friends
```

Note that no output is omitted here. The script only stores information about the people Michel is interested in, but it will always say you are added to the list, unless you are already in it.

Other people can now start executing the script:

```
[anny@octarine tmp]$ friends.sh
Hello, anny.  This script will register you in Michel's friends database.
Enter your name and press [ENTER]: anny
Enter your gender and press [ENTER] :f
How old are you? 22
Which colour of hair do you have? black
You are added to Michel's friends list.
```

After a while, the `friends` list begins to look like this:

```
tille 24 black
anny 22 black
katya 22 blonde
maria 21 black
--output omitted--
```

Of course, this situation is not ideal, since everybody can edit (but not delete) Michel's files. You can solve this problem using special access modes on the script file; see "SUID and SGID" in chapter 4 of the Introduction to Linux guide, <http://tille.soti.org/training/tldp>.

8.2.2 Redirection and file descriptors

As you know from basic shell usage, input and output of a command may be redirected before it is executed, using a special notation - the redirection operators - interpreted by the shell. Redirection may also be used to open and close files for the current shell execution environment.

Redirection can also occur in a script, so that it can receive input from a file, for instance, or send output to a file. Later, the user can review the output file, or it may be used by another script as input.

File input and output are accomplished by integer handles that track all open files for a given process. These numeric values are known as file descriptors. The best known file descriptors are *stdin*, *stdout* and *stderr*, with file descriptor numbers 0, 1 and 2, respectively. These numbers and respective devices are reserved. Bash can take TCP or UDP ports on networked hosts as file descriptors as well.

The output below shows how the reserved file descriptors point to actual devices:

```
michel ~> ls -1 /dev/std*
lrwxrwxrwx 1 root     root     17 Oct  2 07:46 /dev/stderr -> ../proc/self/fd/2
lrwxrwxrwx 1 root     root     17 Oct  2 07:46 /dev/stdin -> ../proc/self/fd/0
lrwxrwxrwx 1 root     root     17 Oct  2 07:46 /dev/stdout -> ../proc/self/fd/1

michel ~> ls -1 /proc/self/fd/[0-2]
lrwx------ 1 michel michel 64 Jan 23 12:11 /proc/self/fd/0 -> /dev/pts/6
lrwx------ 1 michel michel 64 Jan 23 12:11 /proc/self/fd/1 -> /dev/pts/6
lrwx------ 1 michel michel 64 Jan 23 12:11 /proc/self/fd/2 -> /dev/pts/6
```

You might want to check **info MAKEDEV** and **info proc** for more information about /proc subdirectories and the way your system handles standard file descriptors for each running process.

When you run a script from the command line, nothing much changes because the child shell process will use the same file descriptors as the parent. When no such parent is available, for instance when you run a script using the *cron* facility, the standard file descriptors are pipes or other (temporary) files, unless some form of redirection is used. This is demonstrated in the example below, which shows output from a simple **at** script:

```
michel ~> date
Fri Jan 24 11:05:50 CET 2003

michel ~> at 1107
warning: commands will be executed using (in order)
a) $SHELL b) login shell c)/bin/sh
at> ls -1 /proc/self/fd/ > /var/tmp/fdtest.at
at> <EOT>
job 10 at 2003-01-24 11:07

michel ~> cat /var/tmp/fdtest.at
total 0
lr-x------ 1 michel michel 64 Jan 24 11:07 0 -> /var/spool/at/!0000c010959eb \
(deleted)
l-wx------ 1 michel michel 64 Jan 24 11:07 1 -> /var/tmp/fdtest.at
l-wx------ 1 michel michel 64 Jan 24 11:07 2 -> /var/spool/at/spool/a0000c010959eb
lr-x------ 1 michel michel 64 Jan 24 11:07 3 -> /proc/21949/fd
```

And one with **cron**:

```
michel ~> crontab -l
# DO NOT EDIT THIS FILE - edit the master and reinstall.
# (/tmp/crontab.21968 installed on Fri Jan 24 11:30:41 2003)
32 11 * * * ls -1 /proc/self/fd/ > /var/tmp/fdtest.cron
```

```
michel ~> cat /var/tmp/fdtest.cron
total 0
lr-x------ 1 michel michel 64 Jan 24 11:32 0 -> pipe:[124440]
l-wx------ 1 michel michel 64 Jan 24 11:32 1 -> /var/tmp/fdtest.cron
l-wx------ 1 michel michel 64 Jan 24 11:32 2 -> pipe:[124441]
lr-x------ 1 michel michel 64 Jan 24 11:32 3 -> /proc/21974/fd
```

Redirection of errors

From the previous examples, it is clear that you can provide input and output files for a script (see Section 8.2.3 for more), but some tend to forget about redirecting errors - output which might be depended upon later on. Also, if you are lucky, errors will be mailed to you and eventual causes of failure might get revealed. If you are not as lucky, errors will cause your script to fail and won't be caught or sent anywhere, so that you can't start to do any worthwhile debugging.

When redirecting errors, note that the order of precedence is significant. For example, this command, issued in /var/spool

```
ls -l * 2 > /var/tmp/unaccessible-in-spool
```

will redirect output of the **ls** command to the file unaccessible-in-spool in /var/tmp. The command

```
ls -l * > /var/tmp/spoollist 2>&1
```

will direct both standard input and standard error to the file spoollist. The command

```
ls -l * 2>&1 > /var/tmp/spoollist
```

directs only the standard output to the destination file, because the standard error is copied to standard output before the standard output is redirected.

For convenience, errors are often redirected to /dev/null, if it is sure they will not be needed. Hundreds of examples can be found in the startup scripts for your system.

Bash allows for both standard output and standard error to be redirected to the file whose name is the result of the expansion of FILE with this construct:

&> FILE

This is the equivalent of > **FILE 2>&1**, the construct used in the previous set of examples. It is also often combined with redirection to /dev/null, for instance when you just want a command to execute, no matter what output or errors it gives.

8.2.3 File input and output

There are several different ways to read from and write to files from your Bash scripts.

Using /dev/fd

The /dev/fd directory contains entries named 0, 1, 2, and so on. Opening the file /dev/fd/N is equivalent to duplicating file descriptor N. If your system provides /dev/stdin, /dev/stdout and /dev/stderr, you will see that these are equivalent to /dev/fd/0, /dev/fd/1 and /dev/fd/2, respectively.

The main use of the /dev/fd files is from the shell. This mechanism allows for programs that use pathname arguments to handle standard input and standard output in the same way as other pathnames. If /dev/fd is not available on a system, you'll have to find a way to bypass the problem. This can be done for instance using a hyphen (-) to indicate that a program should read from a pipe. An example:

```
michel ~> filter body.txt.gz | cat header.txt - footer.txt
This text is printed at the beginning of each print job and thanks the
sysadmin for setting us up such a great printing infrastructure.

Text to be filtered.

This text is printed at the end of each print job.
```

The **cat** command first reads the file header.txt, next its standard input which is the output of the **filter** command, and last the footer.txt file. The special meaning of the hyphen as a command-line argument to refer to the standard input or standard output is a misconception that has crept into many programs. There might also be problems when specifying hyphen as the first argument, since it might be interpreted as an option to the preceding command. Using /dev/fd allows for uniformity and prevents confusion:

```
michel ~> filter body.txt | cat header.txt /dev/fd/0 footer.txt | lp
```

In this clean example, all output is additionally piped through **lp** to send it to the default printer.

Read and exec

Assigning file descriptors to files Another way of looking at file descriptors is thinking of them as a way to assign a numeric value to a file. Instead of using the file name, you can use the file descriptor number. The **exec** built-in command is used to assign a file descriptor to a file. Use

```
exec fdN> file
```

for assigning file descriptor N to `file` for output, and

```
exec fdN< file
```

for assigning file descriptor N to `file` for input. After a file descriptor has been assigned to a file, it can be used with the shell redirection operators, as is demonstrated in the following example:

```
michel ~> exec 4>result.txt

michel ~> filter body.txt | cat header.txt /dev/fd/0 footer.txt >&4

michel ~> cat result.txt
This text is printed at the beginning of each print job and thanks the
sysadmin for setting us up such a great printing infrastructure.

Text to be filtered.

This text is printed at the end of each print job.
```

 File descriptor 5

Using this file descriptor might cause problems; see the Advanced Bash-Scripting Guide `<http://www.tldp.org/LDP/abs/html/ io-redirection.html>`, chapter 16. You are strongly advised not to use it.

Read in scripts The following is an example that shows how you can alternate between file input and command line input:

```
michel ~/testdir> cat sysnotes.sh
#!/bin/bash

# This script makes an index of important config files, puts them together
# in a backup file and allows for adding comment for each file.

CONFIG=/var/tmp/sysconfig.out
rm "$CONFIG" 2>/dev/null
```

```
echo "Output will be saved in $CONFIG."

exec 7<&0

exec < /etc/passwd

# Read the first line of /etc/passwd
read rootpasswd

echo "Saving root account info..."
echo "Your root account info:" >> "$CONFIG"
echo $rootpasswd >> "$CONFIG"

exec 0<&7 7<&-

echo -n "Enter comment or [ENTER] for no comment: "
read comment; echo $comment >> "$CONFIG"

echo "Saving hosts information..."

# first prepare a hosts file not containing any comments
TEMP="/var/tmp/hosts.tmp"
cat /etc/hosts | grep -v "^#" > "$TEMP"

exec 7<&0
exec < "$TEMP"

read ip1 name1 alias1
read ip2 name2 alias2

echo "Your local host configuration:" >> "$CONFIG"

echo "$ip1 $name1 $alias1" >> "$CONFIG"
echo "$ip2 $name2 $alias2" >> "$CONFIG"

exec 0<&7 7<&-

echo -n "Enter comment or [ENTER] for no comment: "
read comment; echo $comment >> "$CONFIG"
rm "$TEMP"

michel ~/testdir> sysnotes.sh
Output will be saved in /var/tmp/sysconfig.out.

Saving root account info...
Enter comment or [ENTER] for no comment: hint for password: blue lagoon
Saving hosts information...
Enter comment or [ENTER] for no comment: in central DNS

michel ~/testdir> cat /var/tmp/sysconfig.out
Your root account info:
root:x:0:0:root:/root:/bin/bash
hint for password: blue lagoon
Your local host configuration:
127.0.0.1 localhost.localdomain localhost
192.168.42.1 tintagel.kingarthur.com tintagel
in central DNS
```

Closing file descriptors

Since child processes inherit open file descriptors, it is good practice to close a file descriptor when it is no longer needed. This is done using the

```
exec fd<&-
```

syntax. In the above example, file descriptor 7, which has been assigned to standard input, is closed each time the user needs to have access to the actual standard input device, usually the keyboard.

The following is a simple example redirecting only standard error to a pipe:

```
michel ~> cat listdirs.sh
#!/bin/bash

# This script prints standard output unchanged, while standard error is
# redirected for processing by awk.

INPUTDIR="$1"

exec 6>&1

ls "$INPUTDIR"/* 2>&1 >&6 6>&- \
                # Closes fd 6 for awk, but not for ls.

| awk 'BEGIN { FS=":" } { print "YOU HAVE NO ACCESS TO" $2 }' 6>&-

exec 6>&-
```

Here documents

Frequently, your script might call on another program or script that requires input. The *here* document provides a way of instructing the shell to read input from the current source until a line containing only the search string is found (no trailing blanks). All of the lines read up to that point are then used as the standard input for a command.

The result is that you don't need to call on separate files; you can use shell-special characters, and it looks nicer than a bunch of **echo**'s:

```
michel ~> cat startsurf.sh
#!/bin/bash

# This script provides an easy way for users to choose between browsers.

echo "These are the web browsers on this system:"
```

```
# Start here document
cat << BROWSERS
mozilla
links
lynx
konqueror
opera
netscape
BROWSERS
# End here document

echo -n "Which is your favorite? "
read browser

echo "Starting $browser, please wait..."
$browser &

michel ~> startsurf.sh
These are the web browsers on this system:
mozilla
links
lynx
konqueror
opera
netscape
Which is your favorite? opera
Starting opera, please wait...
```

Although we talk about a *here document*, it is supposed to be a construct within the same script. This is an example that installs a package automatically, eventhough you should normally confirm:

```
#!/bin/bash

# This script installs packages automatically, using yum.

if [ $# -lt 1 ]; then
        echo "Usage: $0 package."
        exit 1
fi

yum install $1 << CONFIRM
y
CONFIRM
```

And this is how the script runs. When prompted with the "Is this ok [y/N]" string, the script answers "y" automatically:

```
[root@picon bin]# ./install.sh tuxracer
Gathering header information file(s) from server(s)
Server: Fedora Linux 2 - i386 - core
Server: Fedora Linux 2 - i386 - freshrpms
Server: JPackage 1.5 for Fedora Core 2
Server: JPackage 1.5, generic
Server: Fedora Linux 2 - i386 - updates
Finding updated packages
Downloading needed headers
Resolving dependencies
Dependencies resolved
I will do the following:
[install: tuxracer 0.61-26.i386]
Is this ok [y/N]: <Enter>
Downloading Packages
Running test transaction:
Test transaction complete, Success!
tuxracer 100 % done 1/1
Installed:  tuxracer 0.61-26.i386
Transaction(s) Complete
```

8.3 Summary

In this chapter, we learned how to provide user comments and how to prompt for user input. This is usually done using the **echo/read** combination. We also discussed how files can be used as input and output using file descriptors and redirection, and how this can be combined with getting input from the user.

We stressed the importance of providing ample message for the users of our scripts. As always when others use your scripts, it is better to give too much information than not enough. *Here* documents is a type of shell construct that allows creation of lists, holding choices for the users. This construct can also be used to execute otherwise interactive tasks in the background, without intervention.

8.4 Exercises

These exercises are practical applications of the constructs discussed in this chapter. When writing the scripts, you may test by using a test directory that does not contain too much data. Write each step, then test that portion of code, rather than writing everything at once.

1. Write a script that asks for the user's age. If it is equal to or higher than 16, print a message saying that this user is allowed to drink alcohol. If the user's age is below 16, print a message telling the user how many years he or she has to wait before legally being allowed to drink.

   As an extra, calculate how much beer an 18+ user has drunk statistically (100 liters/year) and print this information for the user.

2. Write a script that takes one file as an argument. Use a *here* document that presents the user with a couple of choices for compressing the file. Possible choices could be **gzip**, **bzip2**, **compress** and **zip**.

3. Write a script called `homebackup` that automates **tar** so the person executing the script always uses the desired options (cvp) and backup destination directory (/var/backups) to make a backup of his or her home directory. Implement the following features:

   - Test for the number of arguments. The script should run without arguments. If any arguments are present, exit after printing a usage message.

   - Determine whether the `backups` directory has enough free space to hold the backup.

   - Ask the user whether a full or an incremental backup is wanted. If the user does not have a full backup file yet, print a message that a full backup will be taken. In case of an incremental backup, only do this if the full backup is not older than a week.

   - Compress the backup using any compression tool. Inform the user that the script is doing this, because it might take some time, during which the user might start worrying if no output appears on the screen.

   - Print a message informing the user about the size of the compressed backup.

   See **info tar** or Introduction to Linux <http://tille.soti.org/training/tldp/>, chapter 9: "Preparing your data" for background information.

4. Write a script called `simple-useradd.sh` that adds a local user to the system. This script should:

- Take only one argument, or else exit after printing a usage message.
- Check /etc/passwd and decide on the first free user ID. Print a message containing this ID.
- Create a private group for this user, checking the /etc/group file. Print a message containing the group ID.
- Gather information from the operator user: a comment describing this user, choice from a list of shells (test for acceptability, else exit printing a message), expiration date for this account, extra groups of which the new user should be a member.
- With the obtained information, add a line to /etc/passwd, /etc/group and /etc/shadow; create the user's home directory (with correct permissions!); add the user to the desired secondary groups.
- Set the password for this user to a default known string.

5. Rewrite the script from Section 7.2 so that it reads input from the user instead of taking it from the first argument.

Chapter 9

Repetitive tasks

Upon completion of this chapter, you will be able to

- *Use **for**, **while** and **until** loops, and decide which loop fits which occasion.*
- *Use the **break** and **continue** Bash built-ins.*
- *Write scripts using the **select** statement.*
- *Write scripts that take a variable number of arguments.*

9.1 The for loop

The **for** loop is the first of the three shell looping constructs. This loop allows for specification of a list of values. A list of commands is executed for each value in the list.

The syntax for this loop is:

```
for NAME [in LIST ]; do COMMANDS; done
```

If **[in LIST]** is not present, it is replaced with **in $@** and **for** executes the **COM-MANDS** once for each positional parameter that is set (see Section 3.2.4 and Section 7.2).

The return status is the exit status of the last command that executes. If no commands are executed because LIST does not expand to any items, the return status is zero.

NAME can be any variable name, although i is used very often. LIST can be any list of words, strings or numbers, which can be literal or generated by any command. The **COMMANDS** to execute can also be any operating system commands, script, program or shell statement. The first time through the loop, NAME is set to the first item in LIST. The second time, its value is set to the second item in the list, and so on. The loop terminates when NAME has taken on each of the values from LIST and no items are left in LIST.

9.1.1 Examples

Using command substitution for specifying LIST items

The first is a command line example, demonstrating the use of a **for** loop that makes a backup copy of each .xml file. After issuing the command, it is safe to start working on your sources:

```
[carol@octarine ~/articles] ls *.xml
file1.xml   file2.xml   file3.xml

[carol@octarine ~/articles] ls *.xml > list

[carol@octarine ~/articles] for i in `cat list`; do cp "$i" "$i".bak; done

[carol@octarine ~/articles] ls *.xml*
file1.xml file1.xml.bak file2.xml file2.xml.bak file3.xml file3.xml.bak
```

This one lists the files in /sbin that are just plain text files, and possibly scripts:

```
for i in `ls /sbin`; do file /sbin/$i | grep ASCII; done
```

Using the content of a variable to specify LIST items

The following is a specific application script for converting HTML files, compliant with a certain scheme, to PHP files. The conversion is done by taking out the first 25 and the last 21 lines, replacing these with two PHP tags that provide header and footer lines:

```
[carol@octarine ~/html] cat html2php.sh
#!/bin/bash
# specific conversion script for my html files to php
LIST="$(ls *.html)"
for i in "$LIST"; do
    NEWNAME=$(ls "$i" | sed -e 's/html/php/')
    cat beginfile > "$NEWNAME"
    cat "$i" | sed -e '1,25d' | tac | sed -e '1,21d'| tac >> "$NEWNAME"
    cat endfile >> "$NEWNAME"
done
```

Since we don't do a line count here, there is no way of knowing the line number from which to start deleting lines until reaching the end. The problem is solved using **tac**, which reverses the lines in a file.

9.2 The while loop

The **while** construct allows for repetitive execution of a list of commands, as long as the command controlling the **while** loop executes successfully (exit status of zero). The syntax is:

```
while CONTROL-COMMAND; do CONSEQUENT-COMMANDS; done
```

CONTROL-COMMAND can be any command(s) that can exit with a success or failure status. The **CONSEQUENT-COMMANDS** can be any program, script or shell construct.

As soon as the **CONTROL-COMMAND** fails, the loop exits. In a script, the command following the **done** statement is executed.

The return status is the exit status of the last **CONSEQUENT-COMMANDS** command, or zero if none was executed.

9.2.1 Examples

Simple example using while

Here is an example for the impatient:

```
#!/bin/bash

# This script opens 4 terminal windows.

i="0"

while [ $i -lt 4 ]
do
xterm &
i=$[$i+1]
done
```

Nested while loops

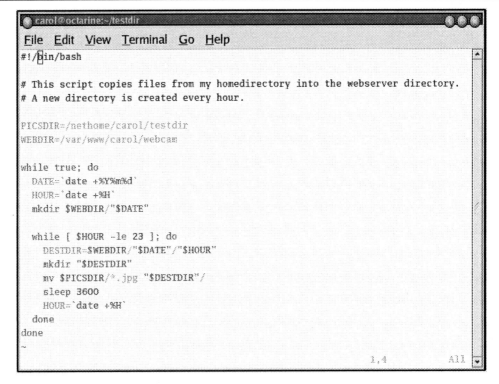

Figure 9.1: Nested while loops - picturesort.sh

The example in Figure 9.1 was written to copy pictures that are made with a web-cam to a web directory. Every five minutes a picture is taken. Every hour, a new directory is created, holding the images for that hour. Every day, a new directory is created containing 24 subdirectories. The script runs in the background.

Note the use of the **true** statement. This means: continue execution until we are forcibly interrupted (with **kill** or **Ctrl+C**).

This small script can be used for simulation testing; it generates files:

```
#!/bin/bash

# This generates a file every 5 minutes

while true; do
touch pic-`date +%s`.jpg
sleep 300
done
```

Note the use of the **date** command to generate all kinds of file and directory names.

Using keyboard input to control the while loop

This script can be interrupted by the user when a **Ctrl+C** sequence is entered:

```
#!/bin/bash

# This script provides wisdom

FORTUNE=/usr/games/fortune

while true; do
echo "On which topic do you want advice?"
cat << topics
politics
startrek
kernelnewbies
sports
bofh-excuses
magic
love
literature
drugs
education
topics
```

```
echo
echo -n "Make your choice: "
read topic
echo
echo "Free advice on the topic of $topic: "
echo
$FORTUNE $topic
echo

done
```

A *here* document is used to present the user with possible choices. And again, the **true** test repeats the commands from the **CONSEQUENT-COMMANDS** list over and over again.

Calculating an average

This script calculates the average of user input, which is tested before it is processed: if input is not within range, a message is printed. If **q** is pressed, the loop exits:

```
#!/bin/bash

# Calculate the average of a series of numbers.

SCORE="0"
AVERAGE="0"
SUM="0"
NUM="0"

while true; do

  echo -n "Enter your score [0-100%] ('q' for quit): "; read SCORE;

  if (("$SCORE" < "0"))  || (("$SCORE" > "100")); then
    echo "Be serious. Common, try again: "
  elif [ "$SCORE" == "q" ]; then
    echo "Average rating: $AVERAGE%."
    break
  else
    SUM=$[$SUM + $SCORE]
    NUM=$[$NUM + 1]
    AVERAGE=$[$SUM / $NUM]
  fi

done

echo "Exiting."
```

Note how the variables in the last lines are left unquoted in order to do arithmetic.

9.3 The until loop

The **until** loop is very similar to the **while** loop, except that the loop executes until the **TEST-COMMAND** executes successfully. As long as this command fails, the loop continues. The syntax is the same as for the **while** loop:

```
until TEST-COMMAND; do CONSEQUENT-COMMANDS; done
```

The return status is the exit status of the last command executed in the **CONSEQUENT-COMMANDS** list, or zero if none was executed. **TEST-COMMAND** can, again, be any command that can exit with a success or failure status, and **CONSEQUENT-COMMANDS** can be any UNIX command, script or shell construct.

As we already explained previously, the ";" may be replaced with one or more newlines wherever it appears.

9.3.1 Example

```
#!/bin/bash

# This script copies files from my homedirectory into the webserver directory.
# A new directory is created every hour.
# If the pics are taking up too much space, the oldest are removed.

PICSDIR=/nethome/carol/testdir
WEBDIR=/var/www/carol/webcam

while true; do
DISKFULL=$(df -h $WEBDIR | grep -v File | awk '{ print $5 }' | cut -d "%" -f1 -)

until [ $DISKFUL -ge "90" ]; do
  DATE=`date +%Y%m%d`
  HOUR=`date +%H`
  mkdir $WEBDIR/"$DATE"

  while [ $HOUR -le 23 ]; do
    DESTDIR=$WEBDIR/"$DATE"/"$HOUR"
    mkdir "$DESTDIR"
    mv $PICSDIR/*.jpg "$DESTDIR"/
    sleep 3600
    HOUR=`date +%H`
  done
  DISKFULL=$(df -h $WEBDIR | grep -v File | awk '{ print $5 }' | cut -d "%" -f1
-)
done

TOREMOVE=$(find $WEBDIR -type d -a -mtime +30)
for i in $TOREMOVE; do rm -rf "$i"; done
[]
done
~
```

Figure 9.2: More nested while loops - safesort.sh

Figure 9.2 shows an improved `picturesort.sh` script (see Section 9.2.1), which tests for available disk space. If not enough disk space is available the script removes pictures from the previous months.

Note the initialization of the HOUR and DISKFULL variables and the use of options with **ls** and **date** in order to obtain a correct listing for TOREMOVE.

9.4 I/O redirection and loops

Instead of controlling a loop by testing the result of a command or by user input, you can specify a file from which to read input that controls the loop. In such cases, **read** is often the controlling command. As long as input lines are fed into the loop, execution of the loop commands continues. As soon as all the input lines are read the loop exits.

Since the loop construct is considered to be one command structure (such as **while TEST-COMMAND; do CONSEQUENT-COMMANDS; done**), the redirection should occur after the **done** statement, so that it complies with the form

```
command < file
```

This kind of redirection also works with other kinds of loops.

9.4.1 Output redirection

In the example below, output of the **find** command is used as input for the **read** command controlling a **while** loop:

```
[carol@octarine ~/testdir] cat archiveoldstuff.sh
#!/bin/bash

# This script creates a subdirectory in the current directory, to which
# old files are moved.
# Might be something for cron (if slightly adapted) to execute weekly or
# monthly.

ARCHIVENR=`date +%Y%m%d`
DESTDIR="$PWD/archive-$ARCHIVENR"

mkdir $DESTDIR

find $PWD -type f -a -mtime +5 | while read file
do
gzip "$file"; mv "$file".gz "$DESTDIR"
echo "$file archived"
done
```

Files are compressed before they are moved into the archive directory.

9.5 Break and continue

The break built-in

The **break** statement is used to exit the current loop before its normal ending. This is done when you don't know in advance how many times the loop will have to execute, for instance because it is dependent on user input.

The example below demonstrates a **while** loop that can be interrupted. This is a slightly improved version of the wisdom.sh script from Section 9.2.1.

```
#!/bin/bash

# This script provides wisdom
# You can now exit in a decent way.

FORTUNE=/usr/games/fortune

while true; do
echo "On which topic do you want advice?"
echo "1.  politics"
echo "2.  startrek"
echo "3.  kernelnewbies"
echo "4.  sports"
echo "5.  bofh-excuses"
echo "6.  magic"
echo "7.  love"
echo "8.  literature"
echo "9.  drugs"
echo "10. education"
echo

echo -n "Enter your choice, or 0 for exit: "
read choice
echo

case $choice in
    1)
    $FORTUNE politics
    ;;
    2)
    $FORTUNE startrek
    ;;
    3)
    $FORTUNE kernelnewbies
    ;;
    4)
    echo "Sports are a waste of time, energy and money."
    echo "Go back to your keyboard."
    echo -e "\t\t\t\t -- \"Unhealthy is my middle name\" Soggie."
    ;;
    5)
    $FORTUNE bofh-excuses
    ;;
    6)
    $FORTUNE magic
    ;;
```

```
        7)
        $FORTUNE love
        ;;
        8)
        $FORTUNE literature
        ;;
        9)
        $FORTUNE drugs
        ;;
        10)
        $FORTUNE education
        ;;
        0)
        echo "OK, see you!"
        break
        ;;
        *)
        echo "That is not a valid choice, try a number from 0 to 10."
        ;;
esac
done
```

Mind that **break** exits the loop, not the script. This can be demonstrated by adding an **echo** command at the end of the script. This **echo** will also be executed upon input that causes **break** to be executed (when the user types "0").

In nested loops, **break** allows for specification of which loop to exit. See the Bash **info** pages for more.

The continue built-in

The **continue** statement resumes iteration of an enclosing **for, while, until** or **select** loop.

When used in a **for** loop, the controlling variable takes on the value of the next element in the list. When used in a **while** or **until** construct, on the other hand, execution resumes with **TEST-COMMAND** at the top of the loop.

9.5.1 Examples

In the following example, file names are converted to lower case. If no conversion needs to be done, a **continue** statement restarts execution of the loop. These commands don't eat much system resources, and most likely, similar problems can be solved using **sed** and **awk**. However, it is useful to know about this kind of construction when executing heavy jobs, that might not even be necessary when tests are inserted at the correct locations in a script, sparing system resources.

```
[carol@octarine ~/test] cat tolower.sh
#!/bin/bash

# This script converts all file names containing upper case characters into
# file names containing only lower case.

LIST="$(ls)"

for name in "$LIST"; do

if [[ "$name" != *[[:upper:]]* ]]; then
continue
fi

ORIG="$name"
NEW=`echo $name | tr 'A-Z' 'a-z'`

mv "$ORIG" "$NEW"
echo "new name for $ORIG is $NEW"
done
```

This script has at least one disadvantage: it overwrites existing files. The no-clobber option to Bash is only useful when redirection occurs. The -b option to the **mv** command provides more security, but is only safe in case of one accidental overwrite, as is demonstrated in this test:

```
[carol@octarine ~/test] rm *

[carol@octarine ~/test] touch test Test TEST

[carol@octarine ~/test] bash -x tolower.sh
++ ls
+ LIST=test
Test
TEST
+ [[ test != *[[:upper:]]* ]]
+ continue
+ [[ Test != *[[:upper:]]* ]]
+ ORIG=Test
++ echo Test
++ tr A-Z a-z
+ NEW=test
+ mv -b Test test
+ echo 'new name for Test is test'
new name for Test is test
+ [[ TEST != *[[:upper:]]* ]]
+ ORIG=TEST
++ echo TEST
++ tr A-Z a-z
+ NEW=test
+ mv -b TEST test
```

```
+ echo 'new name for TEST is test'
new name for TEST is test

[carol@octarine ~/test] ls -a
./  ../  test  test~
```

The **tr** is part of the *textutils* package; it can perform all kinds of character transformations.

9.6 Making menus with the select built-in

Use of select

The **select** construct allows easy menu generation. The syntax is quite similar to that of the **for** loop:

```
select WORD [in LIST]; do RESPECTIVE-COMMANDS; done
```

LIST is expanded, generating a list of items. The expansion is printed to standard error; each item is preceded by a number. If **in LIST** is not present, the positional parameters are printed, as if **in $@** would have been specified. LIST is only printed once.

Upon printing all the items, the PS3 prompt is printed and one line from standard input is read. If this line consists of a number corresponding to one of the items, the value of WORD is set to the name of that item. If the line is empty, the items and the PS3 prompt are displayed again. If an *EOF* (End Of File) character is read, the loop exits. Since most users don't have a clue which key combination is used for the EOF sequence, it is more user-friendly to have a **break** command as one of the items. Any other value of the read line will set WORD to be a null string.

The read line is saved in the REPLY variable.

The **RESPECTIVE-COMMANDS** are executed after each selection until the number representing the **break** is read. This exits the loop.

Examples

This is a very simple example, but as you can see, it is not very user-friendly:

```
[carol@octarine testdir] cat private.sh
#!/bin/bash

echo "This script can make any of the files in this directory private."
echo "Enter the number of the file you want to protect:"

select FILENAME in *;
do
    echo "You picked $FILENAME ($REPLY), it is now only accessible to you."
    chmod go-rwx "$FILENAME"
done
```

```
[carol@octarine testdir] ./private.sh
This script can make any of the files in this directory private.
Enter the number of the file you want to protect:
1) archive-20030129
2) bash
3) private.sh
#? 1
You picked archive-20030129 (1)
#?
```

Setting the PS3 prompt and adding a possibility to quit makes it better:

```
#!/bin/bash

echo "This script can make any of the files in this directory private."
echo "Enter the number of the file you want to protect:"

PS3="Your choice: "
QUIT="QUIT THIS PROGRAM - I feel safe now."
touch "$QUIT"

select FILENAME in *;
do
  case $FILENAME in
        "$QUIT")
           echo "Exiting."
           break
           ;;
        *)
           echo "You picked $FILENAME ($REPLY)"
           chmod go-rwx "$FILENAME"
           ;;
  esac
done
rm "$QUIT"
```

9.6.1 Submenus

Any statement within a **select** construct can be another **select** loop, enabling (a) submenu(s) within a menu.

By default, the PS3 variable is not changed when entering a nested **select** loop. If you want a different prompt in the submenu, be sure to set it at the appropriate time(s).

9.7 The shift built-in

The **shift** command is one of the Bourne shell built-ins that comes with Bash. This command takes one argument, a number. The positional parameters are shifted to the left by this number, N. The positional parameters from N+1 to $# are renamed to variable names from $1 to $# - N+1.

Say you have a command that takes 10 arguments, and N is 4, then $4 becomes $1, $5 becomes $2 and so on. $10 becomes $7 and the original $1, $2 and $3 are thrown away.

If N is zero or greater than $# (the total number of arguments; see Section 7.2). If N is not present, it is assumed to be 1. The return status is zero unless N is greater than $# or less than zero; otherwise it is non-zero.

9.7.1 Examples

A shift statement is typically used when the number of arguments to a command is not known in advance, for instance when users can give as many arguments as they like. In such cases, the arguments are usually processed in a **while** loop with a test condition of **(($#))**. This condition is true as long as the number of arguments is greater than zero. The $1 variable and the **shift** statement process each argument. The number of arguments is reduced each time **shift** is executed and eventually becomes zero, upon which the **while** loop exits.

The example below, cleanup.sh, uses **shift** statements to process each file in the list generated by **find**:

```
#!/bin/bash

# This script can clean up files that were last accessed over 365 days ago.

USAGE="Usage: $0 dir1 dir2 dir3 ... dirN"

if [ "$#" == "0" ]; then
    echo "$USAGE"
    exit 1
fi

while (( "$#" )); do

if [[ "$(ls $1)" == "" ]]; then
    echo "Empty directory, nothing to be done."
    shift
```

```
    else
        find $1 -type f -a -atime +365 -exec rm -i {} \;
fi

shift

done
```

In the next example, we modified the script from Section 8.2.3 so that it accepts multiple packages to install at once:

```
#!/bin/bash
if [ $# -lt 1 ]; then
        echo "Usage: $0 package(s)"
        exit 1
fi
while (($#)); do
    yum install $1 << CONFIRM
    y
    CONFIRM
    shift
done
```

9.8 Summary

In this chapter, we discussed how repetitive commands can be incorporated in loop constructs. Most common loops are built using the **for**, **while** or **until** statements, or a combination of these commands. The **for** loop executes a task a defined number of times. If you don't know how many times a command should execute, use either **until** or **while** to specify when the loop should end.

Loops can be interrupted or reiterated using the **break** and **continue** statements.

A file can be used as input for a loop using the input redirection operator, loops can also read output from commands that is fed into the loop using a pipe.

The **select** construct is used for printing menus in interactive scripts. Looping through the command line arguments to a script can be done using the **shift** statement.

9.9 Exercises

Remember: when building scripts, work in steps and test each step before incorporating it in your script.

1. Create a script that will take a (recursive) copy of files in /etc so that a beginning system administrator can edit files without fear.

2. Write a script that takes exactly one argument, a directory name. If the number of arguments is more or less than one, print a usage message. If the argument is not a directory, print another message. For the given directory, print the five biggest files and the five files that were most recently modified.

3. Can you explain why it is so important to put the variables in between double quotes in the example from Section 9.4.1?

4. Write a script similar to the one in Section 9.5, but think of a way of quitting after the user has executed 3 loops.

5. Think of a better solution than **move -b** for the script from Section 9.5.1 to prevent overwriting of existing files. For instance, test whether or not a file exists. Don't do unnecessary work!

6. Rewrite the whichdaemon.sh script from Section 7.5, so that it:

    - Prints a list of servers to check, such as Apache, the SSH server, the NTP daemon, a name daemon, a power management daemon, and so on.

    - For each choice the user can make, print some sensible information, like the name of the web server, NTP trace information, and so on.

    - Optionally, build in a possibility for users to check other servers than the ones listed. For such cases, check that at least the given process is running.

    - Review the script from Section 9.2.1. Note how character input other than **q** is processed. Rebuild this script so that it prints a message if characters are given as input.

Chapter 10

More on variables

In this chapter, we will discuss the advanced use of variables and arguments. Upon completion, you will be able to:

- *Declare and use an array of variables*
- *Specify the sort of variable you want to use*
- *Make variables read-only*
- *Use **set** to assign a value to a variable*

10.1 Types of variables

As we already saw, Bash understands many different kinds of variables or parameters. Thus far, we haven't bothered much with what kind of variables we assigned, so our variables could hold any value that we assigned to them. A simple command line example demonstrates this:

```
[bob in ~] VARIABLE=12

[bob in ~] echo $VARIABLE
12

[bob in ~] VARIABLE=string

[bob in ~] echo $VARIABLE
string
```

There are cases when you want to avoid this kind of behavior, for instance when handling telephone and other numbers. Apart from integers and variables, you may also want to specify a variable that is a constant. This is often done at the beginning of a script, when the value of the constant is declared. After that, there are only references to the constant variable name, so that when the constant needs to be changed, it only has to be done once. A variable may also be a series of variables of any type, a so-called *array* of variables (VAR0VAR1, VAR2, ... VARN).

10.1.1 Using the declare built-in

Using a **declare** statement, we can limit the value assignment to variables.

The syntax for **declare** is the following:

```
declare OPTION(s) VARIABLE=value
```

The following options are used to determine the type of data the variable can hold and to assign it attributes:

Table 10.1: Options to the declare built-in

Option	Meaning
-a	Variable is an array.
-f	Use function names only.
-i	The variable is to be treated as an integer; arithmetic evaluation is performed when the variable is assigned a value (see Section 3.4.5).
-p	Display the attributes and values of each variable. When -p is used, additional options are ignored.

-r	Make variables read-only. These variables cannot then be assigned values by subsequent assignment statements, nor can they be unset.
-t	Give each variable the *trace* attribute.
-x	Mark each variable for export to subsequent commands via the environment.

Using + instead of - turns off the attribute instead. When used in a function, **declare** creates local variables.

The following example shows how assignment of a type to a variable influences the value.

```
[bob in ~] declare -i VARIABLE=12

[bob in ~] VARIABLE=string

[bob in ~] echo $VARIABLE
0

[bob in ~] declare -p VARIABLE
declare -i VARIABLE="0"
```

Note that Bash has an option to declare a numeric value, but none for declaring string values. This is because, by default, if no specifications are given, a variable can hold any type of data:

```
[bob in ~] OTHERVAR=blah

[bob in ~] declare -p OTHERVAR
declare -- OTHERVAR="blah"
```

As soon as you restrict assignment of values to a variable, it can only hold that type of data. Possible restrictions are either integer, constant or array.

See the Bash info pages for information on return status.

10.1.2 Constants

In Bash, constants are created by making a variable read-only. The **readonly** built-in marks each specified variable as unchangeable. The syntax is:

```
readonly OPTION VARIABLE(s)
```

The values of these variables can then no longer be changed by subsequent assignment. If the -f option is given, each variable refers to a shell function; see Chapter 11, "Functions". If -a is specified, each variable refers to an array of variables. If no arguments are given, or if -p is supplied, a list of all read-only variables is displayed. Using the -p option, the output can be reused as input.

The return status is zero, unless an invalid option was specified, one of the variables or functions does not exist, or -f was supplied for a variable name instead of for a function name.

```
[bob in ~] readonly TUX=penguinpower

[bob in ~] TUX=Mickeysoft
bash: TUX: readonly variable
```

10.2 Array variables

An array is a variable containing multiple values. Any variable may be used as an array. There is no maximum limit to the size of an array, nor any requirement that member variables be indexed or assigned contiguously. Arrays are zero-based: the first element is indexed with the number 0.

Indirect declaration is done using the following syntax to declare a variable:

```
ARRAY[INDEXNR]=value
```

The *INDEXNR* is treated as an arithmetic expression that must evaluate to a positive number.

Explicit declaration of an array is done using the **declare** built-in:

```
declare -a ARRAYNAME
```

A declaration with an index number will also be accepted, but the index number will be ignored. Attributes to the array may be specified using the **declare** and **readonly** built-ins. Attributes apply to all variables in the array; you can't have mixed arrays.

Array variables may also be created using compound assignments in this format:

```
ARRAY=(value1 value2 ...  valueN)
```

Each value is then in the form of *[indexnumber=]string*. The index number is optional. If it is supplied, that index is assigned to it; otherwise the index of the element assigned is the number of the last index that was assigned, plus one. This format is accepted by **declare** as well. If no index numbers are supplied, indexing starts at zero.

Adding missing or extra members in an array is done using the syntax:

```
ARRAYNAME[indexnumber]=value
```

Remember that the **read** built-in provides the -a option, which allows for reading and assigning values for member variables of an array.

10.2.1   Dereferencing the variables in an array

In order to refer to the content of an item in an array, use curly braces. This is necessary, as you can see from the following example, to bypass the shell inter-pretation of expansion operators. If the index number is @ or *, all members of an array are referenced.

```
[bob in ~] ARRAY=(one two three)

[bob in ~] echo ${ARRAY[*]}
one two three

[bob in ~] echo $ARRAY[*]
one[*]

[bob in ~] echo ${ARRAY[2]}
three

[bob in ~] ARRAY[3]=four

[bob in ~] echo ${ARRAY[*]}
one two three four
```

Referring to the content of a member variable of an array without providing an index number is the same as referring to the content of the first element, the one referenced with index number zero.

10.2.2   Deleting array variables

The **unset** built-in is used to destroy arrays or member variables of an array:

```
[bob in ~] unset ARRAY[1]

[bob in ~] echo ${ARRAY[*]}
one three four

[bob in ~] unset ARRAY

[bob in ~] echo ${ARRAY[*]}
<--no output-->
```

10.2.3   Examples of arrays

Practical examples of the usage of arrays are hard to find. You will find plenty of scripts that don't really do anything on your system but that do use arrays to calculate mathematical series, for instance. And that would be one of the more interesting examples...most scripts just show what you can do with an array in an oversimplified and theoretical way.

The reason for this dullness is that arrays are rather complex structures. You will find that most practical examples for which arrays could be used are already implemented on your system using arrays, however on a lower level, in the C programming language in which most UNIX commands are written. A good example is the Bash **history** built-in command. Those readers who are interested might check the built-ins directory in the Bash source tree and take a look at fc.def, which is processed when compiling the built-ins.

Another reason good examples are hard to find is that not all shells support arrays, so they break compatibility.

After long days of searching, I finally found this example operating at an Internet provider. It distributes Apache web server configuration files onto hosts in a web farm:

```
#!/bin/bash

if [ $(whoami) != 'root' ]; then
        echo "Must be root to run $0"
        exit 1;
fi
if [ -z $1 ]; then
        echo "Usage: $0 </path/to/httpd.conf>"
        exit 1
fi

httpd_conf_new=$1
httpd_conf_path="/usr/local/apache/conf"
login=htuser

farm_hosts=(web03 web04 web05 web06 web07)

for i in ${farm_hosts[@]}; do
        su $login -c "scp $httpd_conf_new ${i}:${httpd_conf_path}"
        su $login -c "ssh $i sudo /usr/local/apache/bin/apachectl graceful"

done
exit 0
```

First two tests are performed to check whether the correct user is running the script with the correct arguments. The names of the hosts that need to be configured are listed in the array farm_hosts. Then all these hosts are provided with the Apache configuration file, after which the daemon is restarted. Note the use of commands from the Secure Shell suite, encrypting the connections to remote hosts.

Thanks, Eugene and colleague, for this contribution.

Dan Richter contributed the following example. This is the problem he was confronted with:

"...In my company, we have demos on our web site, and every week someone has to test all of them. So I have a cron job that fills an array with the possible candidates, uses **date +%W** to find the week of the year, and does a modulo operation to find the correct index. The lucky person gets notified by e-mail."

And this was his way of solving it:

```
#!/bin/bash
# This is get-tester-address.sh
#
# First, we test whether bash supports arrays.
# (Support for arrays was only added recently.)
#
whotest[0]='test' || (echo 'Failure: arrays not supported in this version
of bash.' && exit 2)

#
# Our list of candidates. (Feel free to add or
# remove candidates.)
#
wholist=(
    'Bob Smith <bob@example.com>'
    'Jane L. Williams <jane@example.com>'
    'Eric S. Raymond <esr@example.com>'
    'Larry Wall <wall@example.com>'
    'Linus Torvalds <linus@example.com>'
   )
#
# Count the number of possible testers.
# (Loop until we find an empty string.)
#
count=0
while [ "x${wholist[count]}" != "x" ]
do
   count=$(( $count + 1 ))
done


#
# Now we calculate whose turn it is.
#
week=`date '+%W'`       # The week of the year (0..53).
week=${week#0}          # Remove possible leading zero.

let "index = $week % $count"   # week modulo count = the lucky person

email=${wholist[index]}     # Get the lucky person's e-mail address.

echo $email        # Output the person's e-mail address.
```

This script is then used in other scripts, such as this one, which uses a *here* document:

```
email='get-tester-address.sh'   # Find who to e-mail.
hostname='hostname'             # This machine's name.

#
# Send e-mail to the right person.
#
mail $email -s '[Demo Testing]' <<EOF
The lucky tester this week is: $email

Reminder: the list of demos is here:
    http://web.example.com:8080/DemoSites

(This e-mail was generated by $0 on ${hostname}.)
EOF
```

10.3 Operations on variables

Having discussed arithmetic on variables in Section 3.4.5, we now look at some other operations you can perform on Bash variables.

10.3.1 Length of a variable

Using the ${#VAR} syntax will calculate the number of characters in a variable. If VAR is "*" or "@", this value is substituted with the number of positional parameters or number of elements in an array in general. This is demonstrated in the example below:

```
[bob in ~] echo $SHELL
/bin/bash

[bob in ~] echo ${#SHELL}
9

[bob in ~] ARRAY=(one two three)

[bob in ~] echo ${#ARRAY}
3
```

10.3.2 Transformations of variables

Substitution

${VAR:-WORD}

If VAR is not defined or null, the expansion of WORD is substituted; otherwise the value of VAR is substituted:

```
[bob in ~] echo ${TEST:-test}
test

[bob in ~] echo $TEST

[bob in ~] export TEST=a_string

[bob in ~] echo ${TEST:-test}
a_string

[bob in ~] echo ${TEST2:-$TEST}
a_string
```

This form is often used in conditional tests, for instance in this one:

```
[ -z "${COLUMNS:-}" ] && COLUMNS=80
```

It is a shorter notation for

```
if [ -z "${COLUMNS:-}" ]; then
    COLUMNS=80
fi
```

See Section 7.1.1 for more information about this type of condition testing.

If the hyphen (-) is replaced with the equal sign (=), the value is assigned to the parameter if it does not exist:

```
[bob in ~] echo $TEST2

[bob in ~] echo ${TEST2:=$TEST}
a_string

[bob in ~] echo $TEST2
a_string
```

The following syntax tests the existence of a variable. If it is not set, the expansion of *WORD* is printed to standard out and non-interactive shells quit. A demonstration:

```
[bob in ~] cat vartest.sh
#!/bin/bash

# This script tests whether a variable is set.  If not,
# it exits printing a message.

echo ${TESTVAR:?"There's so much I still wanted to do..."}
echo "TESTVAR is set, we can proceed."

[bob in testdir] ./vartest.sh
./vartest.sh: line 6: TESTVAR: There's so much I still wanted to do...

[bob in testdir] export TESTVAR=present

[bob in testdir] ./vartest.sh
present
TESTVAR is set, we can proceed.
```

Using "+" instead of the exclamation mark sets the variable to the expansion of *WORD*; if it does not exist, nothing happens.

Removing substrings

To strip a number of characters, equal to *OFFSET*, from a variable, use this syntax:

${VAR: *OFFSET*: *LENGTH*}

The *LENGTH* parameter defines how many characters to keep, starting from the first character after the offset point. If *LENGTH* is omitted, the remainder of the variable content is taken:

```
[bob in ~] export STRING="thisisaverylongname"

[bob in ~] echo ${STRING:4}
isaverylongname

[bob in ~] echo ${STRING:6:5}
avery
```

${VAR#*WORD*}

and

${VAR##*WORD*}

These constructs are used for deleting the pattern matching the expansion of *WORD* in VAR. *WORD* is expanded to produce a pattern just as in file name expansion. If the pattern matches the beginning of the expanded value of VAR, then the result of the expansion is the expanded value of VAR with the shortest matching pattern ("#") or the longest matching pattern (indicated with "##").

If VAR is * or @, the pattern removal operation is applied to each positional parameter in turn, and the expansion is the resultant list.

If VAR is an array variable subscribed with "*" or "*", the pattern removal operation is applied to each member of the array in turn, and the expansion is the resultant list. This is shown in the examples below:

```
[bob in ~] echo ${ARRAY[*]}
one two one three one four

[bob in ~] echo ${ARRAY[*]#one}
two three four

[bob in ~] echo ${ARRAY[*]#t}
one wo one hree one four

[bob in ~] echo ${ARRAY[*]#t*}
one wo one hree one four

[bob in ~] echo ${ARRAY[*]##t*}
one one one four
```

The opposite effect is obtained using "%" and "%%", as in this example below. *WORD* should match a trailing portion of string:

```
[bob in ~] echo $STRING
thisisaverylongname

[bob in ~] echo ${STRING%name}
thisisaverylong
```

Replacing parts of variable names

This is done using the

${VAR/*PATTERN*/*STRING*}

or

${VAR//*PATTERN*/*STRING*}

syntax. The first form replaces only the first match, the second replaces all matches of *PATTERN* with *STRING*:

```
[bob in ~] echo ${STRING/name/string}
thisisaverylongstring
```

More information can be found in the Bash info pages.

10.4 Summary

Normally, a variable can hold any type of data, unless variables are declared explicitly. Constant variables are set using the **readonly** built-in command.

An array holds a set of variables. If a type of data is declared, then all elements in the array will be set to hold only this type of data.

Bash features allow for substitution and transformation of variables "on the fly". Standard operations include calculating the length of a variable, arithmetic on variables, substituting variable content and substituting part of the content.

10.5 Exercises

Here are some brain crackers:

1. Write a script that does the following:

    - Display the name of the script being executed.
    - Display the first, third and tenth argument given to the script.
    - Display the total number of arguments passed to the script.
    - If there were more than three positional parameters, use **shift** to move all the values 3 places to the left.
    - Print all the values of the remaining arguments.
    - Print the number of arguments.

    Test with zero, one, three and over ten arguments.

2. Write a script that implements a simple web browser (in text mode), using **wget** and **links -dump** to display HTML pages to the user. The user has 3 choices: enter a URL, enter **b** for back and **q** to quit. The last 10 URLs entered by the user are stored in an array, from which the user can restore the URL by using the *back* functionality.

Chapter 11

Functions

In this chapter, we will discuss

- *What functions are*
- *Creation and displaying of functions from the command line*
- *Functions in scripts*
- *Passing arguments to functions*
- *When to use functions*

11.1 What are functions?

Shell functions are a way to group commands for later execution, using a single name for this group, or *routine*. The name of the routine must be unique within the shell or script. All the commands that make up a function are executed like regular commands. When calling on a function as a simple command name, the list of commands associated with that function name is executed. A function is executed within the shell in which it has been declared: no new process is created to interpret the commands.

Special built-in commands are found before shell functions during command lookup. The special built-ins are: **break**, **:**, **.**, **continue**, **eval**, **exec**, **exit**, **export**, **readonly**, **return**, **set**, **shift**, **trap** and **unset**.

11.1.1 Function syntax

Functions either use the syntax

```
function FUNCTION { COMMANDS; }
```

or

```
FUNCTION () { COMMANDS; }
```

Both define a shell function **FUNCTION**. The use of the built-in command **function** is optional; however, if it is not used, parentheses are needed.

The commands listed between curly braces make up the body of the function. These commands are executed whenever **FUNCTION** is specified as the name of a command. The exit status is the exit status of the last command executed in the body.

 Common mistakes

The curly braces must be separated from the body by spaces, otherwise they are interpreted in the wrong way.

The body of a function should end in a semicolon or a newline.

11.1.2 Positional parameters in functions

Functions are like mini-scripts: they can accept parameters, they can use variables only known within the function (using the **local** shell built-in) and they can return values to the calling shell.

A function also has a system for interpreting positional parameters. However, the positional parameters passed to a function are not the same as the ones passed to a command or script.

When a function is executed, the arguments to the function become the positional parameters during its execution. The special parameter # that expands to the number of positional parameters is updated to reflect the change. Positional parameter 0 is unchanged. The Bash variable FUNCNAME is set to the name of the function, while it is executing.

If the **return** built-in is executed in a function, the function completes and execution resumes with the next command after the function call. When a function completes, the values of the positional parameters and the special parameter # are restored to the values they had prior to the function's execution. If a numeric argument is given to **return**, that status is returned. A simple example:

```
[lydia@cointreau ~/test] cat showparams.sh
#!/bin/bash

echo "This script demonstrates function arguments."
echo

echo "Positional parameter 1 for the script is $1."
echo

test ()
{
echo "Positional parameter 1 in the function is $1."
RETURN_VALUE=$?
echo "The exit code of this function is $RETURN_VALUE."
}

test other_param

[lydia@cointreau ~/test] ./showparams.sh parameter1
This script demonstrates function arguments.

Positional parameter 1 for the script is parameter1.

Positional parameter 1 in the function is other_param.
The exit code of this function is 0.

[lydia@cointreau ~/test]
```

Note that the return value or exit code of the function is often storen in a variable, so that it can be probed at a later point. The init scripts on your system often use the technique of probing the RETVAL variable in a conditional test, like this one:

```
if [ $RETVAL -eq 0 ]; then
    <start the daemon>
```

Or like this example from the /etc/init.d/amd script, where Bash's optimazation features are used:

```
[ $RETVAL = 0 ] && touch /var/lock/subsys/amd
```

The commands after **&&** are only executed when the test proves to be true; this is a shorter way to represent an **if/then/fi** structure.

The return code of the function is often used as exit code of the entire script. You'll see a lot of initscripts ending in something like **exit $RETVAL**.

11.1.3   Displaying functions

All functions known by the current shell can be displayed using the **set** built-in without options. Functions are retained after they are used, unless they are **unset** after use. The **which** command also displays functions:

```
[lydia@cointreau ~] which zless
zless is a function
zless ()
{
    zcat "$@" | "$PAGER"
}

[lydia@cointreau ~] echo $PAGER
less
```

This is the sort of function that is typically configured in the user's shell resource configuration files. Functions are more flexible than aliases and provide a simple and easy way of adapting the user environment.

Here's one for DOS users:

```
dir ()
{
    ls -F --color=auto -1F --color=always "$@" | less -r
}
```

11.2 Examples of functions in scripts

11.2.1 Recycling

There are plenty of scripts on your system that use functions as a structured way of handling series of commands. On some Linux systems, for instance, you will find the /etc/rc.d/init.d/functions definition file, which is sourced in all init scripts. Using this method, common tasks such as checking if a process runs, starting or stopping a daemon and so on, only have to be written once, in a general way. If the same task is needed again, the code is recycled. From this functions file the **checkpid** function:

```
# Check if $pid (could be plural) are running
checkpid() {
        local i

        for i in $* ; do
                [ -d "/proc/$i" ] && return 0
        done
        return 1
}
```

This function is reused in the same script in other functions, which are reused in other scripts. The **daemon** function, for instance, is used in the majority of the startup scripts for starting a server process (on machines that use this system).

11.2.2 Setting the path

This section might be found in your /etc/profile file. The function **pathmunge** is defined and then used to set the path for the *root* and other users:

```
pathmunge () {
        if ! echo $PATH | /bin/egrep -q "(^|:)$1($|:)" ; then
            if [ "$2" = "after" ] ; then
                PATH=$PATH:$1
            else
                PATH=$1:$PATH
            fi
        fi
}
# Path manipulation
if [ `id -u` = 0 ]; then
        pathmunge /sbin
        pathmunge /usr/sbin
```

```
        pathmunge /usr/local/sbin
fi

pathmunge /usr/X11R6/bin after

unset pathmunge
```

The function takes its first argument to be a path name. If this path name is not yet in the current path, it is added. The second argument to the function defines if the path will be added in front or after the current PATH definition.

Normal users only get /usr/X11R6/bin added to their paths, while *root* gets a couple of extra directories containing system commands. After being used, the function is unset so that it is not retained.

11.2.3 Remote backups

The following example is one that I use for making backups of the files for my books. It uses SSH keys for enabling the remote connection. Two functions are defined, **buplinux** and **bupbash**, that each make a .tar file, which is then compressed and sent to a remote server. After that, the local copy is cleaned up.

On Sunday, only **bupbash** is executed.

```
#/bin/bash

LOGFILE="/nethome/tille/log/backupscript.log"
echo "Starting backups for `date`" >> "$LOGFILE"

buplinux()
{
DIR="/nethome/tille/xml/db/linux-basics/"
TAR="Linux.tar"
BZIP="$TAR.bz2"
SERVER="rincewind"
RDIR="/var/www/intra/tille/html/training/"

cd "$DIR"
tar cf "$TAR" src/*.xml src/images/*.png src/images/*.eps
echo "Compressing $TAR..." >> "$LOGFILE"
bzip2 "$TAR"
echo "...done." >> "$LOGFILE"
echo "Copying to $SERVER..." >> "$LOGFILE"
scp "$BZIP" "$SERVER:$RDIR" > /dev/null 2>&1
echo "...done." >> "$LOGFILE"
echo -e "Done backing up Linux course:\nSource files, PNG and EPS images. \
\nRubbish removed." >> "$LOGFILE"
rm "$BZIP"
}
```

```
bupbash()
{
DIR="/nethome/tille/xml/db/"
TAR="Bash.tar"
BZIP="$TAR.bz2"
FILES="bash-programming/"
SERVER="rincewind"
RDIR="/var/www/intra/tille/html/training/"

cd "$DIR"
tar cf "$TAR" "$FILES"
echo "Compressing $TAR..." >> "$LOGFILE"
bzip2 "$TAR"
echo "...done." >> "$LOGFILE"
echo "Copying to $SERVER..." >> "$LOGFILE"
scp "$BZIP" "$SERVER:$RDIR" > /dev/null 2>&1
echo "...done." >> "$LOGFILE"

echo -e "Done backing up Bash course:\n$FILES\nRubbish removed." >> "$LOGFILE"
rm "$BZIP"
}

DAY=`date +%w`

if [ "$DAY" -lt "2" ]; then
  echo "It is `date +%A`, only backing up Bash course." >> "$LOGFILE"
  bupbash
else
  buplinux
  bupbash
fi

echo -e "Remote backup `date` SUCCESS\n----------" >> "$LOGFILE"
```

This script runs from cron, meaning without user interaction, so we redirect standard error from the **scp** command to /dev/null.

It might be argued that all the separate steps can be combined in a command such as

```
tar c dir_to_backup/ | bzip2 | ssh server "cat > backup.
tar.bz2"
```

However, if you are interested in intermediate results, which might be recovered upon failure of the script, this is not what you want.

The expression

```
command &> file
```

is equivalent to

```
command > file 2>&1
```

11.3 Summary

Functions provide an easy way of grouping commands that you need to execute repetitively. When a function is running, the positional parameters are changed to those of the function. When it stops, they are reset to those of the calling program. Functions are like mini-scripts, and just like a script, they generate exit or return codes.

While this was a short chapter, it contains important knowledge needed for achieving the ultimate state of laziness that is the typical goal of any system administrator.

11.4 Exercises

Here are some useful things you can do using functions:

1. Add a function to your ~/.bashrc config file that automates the printing of man pages. The result should be that you type something like **printman <command>**, upon which the first appropriate man page rolls out of your printer. Check using a pseudo printer device for testing purposes.

   As an extra, build in a possibility for the user to supply the section number of the man page he or she wants to print.

2. Create a subdirectory in your home directory in which you can store function definitions. Put a couple of functions in that directory. Useful functions might be, amongst others, that you have the same commands as on DOS or a commercial UNIX when working with Linux, or vice versa. These functions should then be imported in your shell environment when ~/.bashrc is read.

Chapter 12

Catching signals

In this chapter, we will discuss the following subjects:

- *Available signals*
- *Use of the signals*
- *Use of the **trap** statement*
- *How to prevent users from interrupting your programs*

12.1 Signals

 ### Finding the signal man page

Your system contains a man page listing all the available signals, but depending on your operating system, it might be opened in a different way. On most Linux systems, this will be **man 7 signal**. When in doubt, locate the exact man page and section using commands like

```
man -k signal | grep list
```

or

```
apropos signal | grep list
```

Signal names can be found using **kill -l**.

Signals to your Bash shell

In the absence of any traps, an interactive Bash shell ignores *SIGTERM* and *SIGQUIT*. *SIGINT* is caught and handled, and if job control is active, *SIGTTIN*, *SIGTTOU* and *SIGTSTP* are also ignored. Commands that are run as the result of a command substitution also ignore these signals, when keyboard generated.

SIGHUP by default exits a shell. An interactive shell will send a *SIGHUP* to all jobs, running or stopped; see the documentation on the **disown** built-in if you want to disable this default behavior for a particular process. Use the `huponexit` option for killing all jobs upon receiving a *SIGHUP* signal, using the **shopt** built-in.

Sending signals using the shell

Table 12.1 lists the signals can be sent using the Bash shell.

 ### Terminal settings

Check your **stty** settings. Suspend and resume of output is usually disabled if you are using "modern" terminal emulations. The standard **xterm** supports **Ctrl+S** and **Ctrl+Q** by default.

12.1.1 Usage of signals with kill

Most modern shells, Bash included, have a built-in **kill** function. In Bash, both signal names and numbers are accepted as options, and arguments may be job

Table 12.1: Control signals in Bash

Standard key combination	Meaning
Ctrl+C	The interrupt signal.
Ctrl+S	Suspend output (XOFF)
Ctrl+Q	Resume output (XON)
Ctrl+Y	The *delayed suspend* character. Causes a running process to be stopped when it attempts to read input from the terminal. Control is returned to the shell, the user can foreground, background or kill the process.
Ctrl+Z	The *suspend* character. Stops a running program and returns control to the shell.

or process IDs. An exit status can be reported using the -1 option: zero when at least one signal was successfully sent, non-zero if an error occurred.

Using the **kill** command from /usr/bin, your system might enable extra options, such as the ability to kill processes from other than your own user ID and specifying processes by name, like with **pgrep** and **pkill**.

Both **kill** commands send the *TERM* signal if none is given.

This is a list of the most common signals:

Table 12.2: Common kill signals

Signal name	Signal value	Effect
SIGHUP	1	Hangup
SIGINT	2	Interrupt from keyboard
SIGKILL	9	Kill signal
SIGTERM	15	Termination signal
SIGSTOP	17,19,23	Stop the process

 SIGKILL and SIGSTOP

SIGKILL and *SIGSTOP* can not be caught, blocked or ignored.

When killing a process or series of processes, it is common sense to start trying with the least dangerous signal, *SIGTERM*. If that does not work, use the *INT* or*KILL* signals. For instance, when a process does not die using **Ctrl+C**, it is best to use the **kill -9** on that process ID:

```
maud: ~> ps -ef | grep stuck_process
maud     5607   2214  0 20:05 pts/5     00:00:02 stuck_process

maud: ~> kill -9 5607

maud: ~> ps -ef | grep stuck_process
maud     5614   2214 0 20:15 pts/5      00:00:00 grep stuck_process
[1]+ Killed      stuck_process
```

When a process starts up several instances, **killall** might be easier. It takes the same option as the **kill** command, but applies on all instances of a given process. Test this command before using it in a production environment, since it might not work as expected on some of the commercial Unices.

12.2 Traps

There might be situations when you don't want users of your scripts to exit untimely using keyboard abort sequences, for example because input has to be provided or cleanup has to be done. The **trap** statement catches these sequences and can be programmed to execute a list of commands upon catching those signals.

The syntax for the **trap** statement is straightforward:

```
trap [COMMANDS] [SIGNALS]
```

This instructs the **trap** command to catch the listed *SIGNALS*, which may be signal names with or without the *SIG* prefix, or signal numbers. If a signal is *0* or *EXIT*, the **COMMANDS** are executed when the shell exits. If one of the signals is *DEBUG*, the list of **COMMANDS** is executed after every simple command. A signal may also be specified as *ERR*; in that case **COMMANDS** are executed each time a simple command exits with a non-zero status. Note that these commands will not be executed when the non-zero exit status comes from part of an **if** statement, or from a **while** or **until** loop. Neither will they be executed if a logical *AND* (&&) or *OR* (||) result in a non-zero exit code, or when a command's return status is inverted using the *!* operator.

The return status of the **trap** command itself is zero unless an invalid signal specification is encountered. The **trap** command takes a couple of options, which are documented in the Bash info pages.

Here is a very simple example, catching **Ctrl+C** from the user, upon which a message is printed. When you try to kill this program without specifying the *KILL* signal, nothing will happen:

```
#!/bin/bash
# traptest.sh

trap "echo Booh!" SIGINT SIGTERM
echo "pid is $$"

while :               # This is the same as "while true".
do
        sleep 60      # This script is not really doing anything.
done
```

12.2.1 How Bash interprets traps

When Bash receives a signal for which a trap has been set while waiting for a command to complete, the trap will not be executed until the command completes. When Bash is waiting for an asynchronous command via the **wait** built-in, the reception of a signal for which a trap has been set will cause the **wait** built-in to return immediately with an exit status greater than 128, immediately after which the trap is executed.

12.2.2 More examples

Detecting when a variable is used

When debugging longer scripts, you might want to give a variable the *trace* attribute and trap *DEBUG* messages for that variable. Normally you would just declare a variable using an assignment like **VARIABLE=value**. Replacing the declaration of the variable with the following lines might provide valuable information about what your script is doing:

```
declare -t VARIABLE=value

trap "echo VARIABLE is being used here." DEBUG

# rest of the script
```

Removing rubbish upon exit

The **whatis** command relies on a database which is regularly built using the makewhatis.cron script with cron:

```
#!/bin/bash

LOCKFILE=/var/lock/makewhatis.lock

# Previous makewhatis should execute successfully:

[ -f $LOCKFILE ] && exit 0

# Upon exit, remove lockfile.

trap "{ rm -f $LOCKFILE ; exit 255; }" EXIT

touch $LOCKFILE
makewhatis -u -w
exit 0
```

12.3 Summary

Signals can be sent to your programs using the **kill** command or keyboard short-cuts. These signals can be caught, upon which action can be performed, using the **trap** statement.

Some programs ignore signals. The only signal that no program can ignore is the *KILL* signal.

12.4 Exercises

A couple of practical examples:

1. Create a script that writes a boot image to a diskette using the **dd** utility. If the user tries to interrupt the script using **Ctrl+C**, display a message that this action will make the diskette unusable.

2. Write a script that automates the installation of a third-party package of your choice. The package must be downloaded from the Internet. It must be de-compressed, unarchived and compiled if these actions are appropriate. Only the actual installation of the package should be uninterruptable.

Appendix A

Shell Features

This document gives an overview of common shell features (the same in every shell flavour) and differing shell features (shell specific features).

A.1 Common features

The following features are standard in every shell. Note that the stop, suspend, jobs, bg and fg commands are only available on systems that support job control.

A.2 Differing features

The table below shows major differences between the standard shell (**sh**), Bourne Again SHell (**bash**), Korn shell (**ksh**) and the C shell (**csh**).

 Shell compatibility

Since the Bourne Again SHell is a superset of **sh**, all **sh** commands will also work in **bash** - but not vice versa. **bash** has many more features of its own, and, as the table below demonstrates, many features incorporated from other shells.

Since the Turbo C shell is a superset of **csh**, all **csh** commands will work in **tcsh**, but not the other way round.

The Bourne Again SHell has many more features not listed here. This table is just to give you an idea of how this shell incorporates all useful ideas from other shells: there are no blanks in the column for **bash**. More information on features found only in Bash can be retrieved from the Bash info pages, in the "Bash Features" section.

More information:

You should at least read one manual, being the manual of your shell. The preferred choice would be **info bash**, **bash** being the GNU shell and easiest for beginners. Print it out and take it home, study it whenever you have 5 minutes.

Table A.1: Common Shell Features

Command	Meaning
>	Redirect output
>>	Append to file
<	Redirect input
<<	"Here" document (redirect input)
|	Pipe output
&	Run process in background.
;	Separate commands on same line
*	Match any character(s) in filename
?	Match single character in filename
[ ]	Match any characters enclosed
( )	Execute in subshell
` `	Substitute output of enclosed command
" "	Partial quote (allows variable and command expansion)
' '	Full quote (no expansion)
\	Quote following character
$var	Use value for variable
$$	Process id
$0	Command name
$n	nth argument (n from 0 to 9)
$*	All arguments as a simple word
#	Begin comment
bg	Background execution
break	Break from loop statements
cd	Change directories
continue	Resume a program loop
echo	Display output
eval	Evaluate arguments
exec	Execute a new shell
fg	Foreground execution
jobs	Show active jobs
kill	Terminate running jobs
newgrp	Change to a new group
shift	Shift positional parameters
stop	Suspend a background job
suspend	Suspend a foreground job
time	Time a command
umask	Set or list file permissions
unset	Erase variable or function definitions
wait	Wait for a background job to finish

Table A.2: Differing Shell Features

sh	bash	ksh	csh	Meaning/Action
$	$	$	%	Default user prompt
	>|	>|	>!	Force redirection
> file 2>&1	&> file or > file 2>&1	> file 2>&1	>& file	Redirect stdout and stderr to file
	{ }		{ }	Expand elements in list
'command'	'command' or $(command)	$(command)	'command'	Substitute output of enclosed **command**
$HOME	$HOME	$HOME	$home	Home directory
	~	~	~	Home directory symbol
	~+, ~-, **dirs**	~+, ~-	=-, =N	Access directory stack
var=value	VAR=value	var=value	set var=value	Variable assignment
export var	export VAR=value	export var=val	setenv var val	Set environment variable
	${nnnn}	${nn}		More than 9 arguments can be referenced
"$@"	"$@"	"$@"		All arguments as separate words
$#	$#	$#	$#argv	Number of arguments
$?	$?	$?	$status	Exit status of the most recently executed command
$!	$!	$!		PID of most recently backgrounded process
$-	$-	$-		Current options
. file	source file or . file	. file	source file	Read commands in file
	alias x='y'	alias x=y	alias x y	Name **x** stands for command **y**
case	case	case	switch or case	Choose alternatives
done	done	done	end	End a loop statement
esac	esac	esac	endsw	End **case** or **switch**
exit n	exit n	exit n	exit (expr)	Exit with a status
for/do	for/do	for/do	foreach	Loop through variables
	set -f, set -o nullglob|dotglob|nocaseglob|noglob		noglob	Ignore substitution characters for filename generation
hash	hash	alias -t	hashstat	Display hashed commands (tracked aliases)
hash cmds	hash cmds	alias -t cmds	rehash	Remember command locations
hash -r	hash -r		unhash	Forget command locations
	history	history	history	List previous commands
	ArrowUp+Enter or !!	r	!!	Redo previous command
	!str	r str	!str	Redo last command that starts with "str"
	!cmd:s/x/y/	r x=y cmd	!cmd:s/x/y/	Replace "x" with "y" in most recent command starting with "cmd", then execute.
if [$i -eq 5]	if [$i -eq 5]	if ((i==5))	if ($i==5)	Sample condition test
fi	fi	fi	endif	End **if** statement
ulimit	ulimit	ulimit	limit	Set resource limits
pwd	pwd	pwd	dirs	Print working directory
read	read	read	$<	Read from terminal
trap 2	trap 2	trap 2	onintr	Ignore interrupts
	unalias	unalias	unalias	Remove aliases
until	until	until		Begin **until** loop
while/do	while/do	while/do	while	Begin **while** loop

Common UNIX Commands

This section contains an alphabetical overview of common UNIX commands. More information about the usage can be found in the man or info pages.

A

a2ps Format files for printing on a PostScript printer.

acroread PDF viewer.

adduser Create a new user or update default new user information.

alias Create a shell alias for a command.

anacron Execute commands periodically, does not assume continuously running machine.

apropos Search the whatis database for strings.

apt-get APT package handling utility.

aspell Spell checker.

at, atq, atrm Queue, examine or delete jobs for later execution.

aumix Adjust audio mixer.

(g)awk Pattern scanning and processing language.

B

bash Bourne Again SHell.

batch Queue, examine or delete jobs for later execution.

bg Run a job in the background.

bitmap Bitmap editor and converter utilities for the X window System.

bzip2 A block-sorting file compressor.

C

cat Concatenate files and print to standard output.

cd Change directory.

cdp/cdplay An interactive text-mode program for controlling and playing audio CD Roms under Linux.

cdparanoia An audio CD reading utility which includes extra data verification features.

cdrecord Record a CD-R.

chattr Change file attributes.

chgrp Change group ownership.

chkconfig Update or query run level information for system services.

chmod Change file access permissions.

chown Change file owner and group.

compress Compress files.

cp Copy files and directories.

crontab Maintain crontab files.

csh Open a C shell.

cut Remove sections from each line of file(s).

D

date Print or set system date and time.

dd Convert and copy a file (disk dump).

df Report file system disk usage.

dhcpcd DHCP client daemon.

diff Find differences between two files.

dig Send domain name query packets to name servers.

dmesg Print or control the kernel ring buffer.

du Estimate file space usage.

E

echo Display a line of text.

ediff Diff to English translator.

egrep Extended grep.

eject Unmount and eject removable media.

emacs Start the Emacs editor.

exec Invoke subprocess(es).

exit Exit current shell.

export Add function(s) to the shell environment.

F

fax2ps Convert a TIFF facsimile to PostScript.

fdformat Format floppy disk.

fdisk Partition table manipulator for Linux.

fetchmail Fetch mail from a POP, IMAP, ETRN or ODMR-capable server.

fg Bring a job in the foreground.

file Determine file type.

find Find files.

formail Mail (re)formatter.

fortune Print a random, hopefully interesting adage.

ftp Transfer files (unsafe unless anonymous account is used!)services.

G

galeon Graphical web browser.

gdm Gnome Display Manager.

(min/a)getty Control console devices.

gimp Image manipulation program.

grep Print lines matching a pattern.

groff Emulate nroff command with groff.

grub The grub shell.

gv A PostScript and PDF viewer.

gzip Compress or expand files.

H

halt Stop the system.

head Output the first part of files.

help Display help on a shell built-in command.

host DNS lookup utility.

httpd Apache hypertext transfer protocol server.

I

id Print real and effective UIDs and GIDs.

ifconfig Configure network interface or show configuration.

info Read Info documents.

init Process control initialization.

iostat Display I/O statistics.

ip Display/change network interface status.

ipchains IP firewall administration.

iptables IP packet filter administration.

J

jar Java archive tool.

jobs List backgrounded tasks.

K

kdm Desktop manager for KDE.

kill(all) Terminate process(es).

ksh Open a Korn shell.

L

ldapmodify Modify an LDAP entry.

ldapsearch LDAP search tool.

less **more** with features.

lilo Linux boot loader.

links Text mode WWW browser.

ln Make links between files.

loadkeys Load keyboard translation tables.

locate Find files.

logout Close current shell.

lp Send requests to the LP print service.

lpc Line printer control program.

lpq Print spool queue examination program.

lpr Offline print.

lprm Remove print requests.

ls List directory content.

lynx Text mode WWW browser.

M

mail Send and receive mail.

man Read man pages.

mcopy Copy MSDOS files to/from Unix.

mdir Display an MSDOS directory.

memusage Display memory usage.

memusagestat Display memory usage statistics.

mesg Control write access to your terminal.

mformat Add an MSDOS file system to a low-level formatted floppy disk.

mkbootdisk Creates a stand-alone boot floppy for the running system.

mkdir Create directory.

mkisofs Create a hybrid ISO9660 filesystem.

more Filter for displaying text one screen at the time.

mount Mount a file system or display information about mounted file systems.

mozilla Web browser.

mt Control magnetic tape drive operation.

mtr Network diagnostic tool.

mv Rename files.

N

named Internet domain name server.

ncftp Browser program for ftp services (insecure!).

netstat Print network connections, routing tables, interface statistics, masquerade connections, and multi-cast memberships.

nfsstat Print statistics about networked file systems.

nice Run a program with modified scheduling priority.

nmap Network exploration tool and security scanner.

ntsysv Simple interface for configuring run levels.

P

passwd Change password.

pdf2ps Ghostscript PDF to PostScript translator.

perl Practical Extraction and Report Language.

pg Page through text output.

ping Send echo request to a host.

pr Convert text files for printing.

printenv Print all or part of environment.

procmail Autonomous mail processor.

ps Report process status.

pstree Display a tree of processes.

pwd Print present working directory.

Q

quota Display disk usage and limits.

R

rcp Remote copy (unsafe!)

rdesktop Remote Desktop Protocol client.

reboot Stop and restart the system.

renice Alter priority of a running process.

rlogin Remote login (telnet, insecure!).

rm Remove a file.

rmdir Remove a directory.

roff A survey of the roff typesetting system.

rpm RPM Package Manager.

rsh Remote shell (insecure!).

S

scp Secure remote copy.

screen Screen manager with VT100 emulation.

set Display, set or change variable.

setterm Set terminal attributes.

sftp Secure (encrypted) ftp.

sh Open a standard shell.

shutdown Bring the system down.

sleep Wait for a given period.

slocate Security Enhanced version of the GNU Locate.

slrnn text mode Usenet client.

snort Network intrusion detection tool.

sort Sort lines of text files.

ssh Secure shell.

ssh-keygen Authentication key generation.

stty Change and print terminal line settings.

su Switch user.

T

tac Concatenate and print files in reverse.

tail Output the last part of files.

talk Talk to a user.

tar Archiving utility.

tcsh Open a Turbo C shell.

telnet User interface to the TELNET protocol (insecure!).

tex Text formatting and typesetting.

time Time a simple command or give resource usage.

tin News reading program.

top Display top CPU processes.

touch Change file timestamps.

traceroute Print the route packets take to network host.

tripwire A file integrity checker for UNIX systems.

troff Format documents.

twm Tab Window Manager for the X Window System.

U

ulimit Controll resources.

umask Set user file creation mask.

umount Unmount a file system.

uncompress Decompress compressed files.

uniq Remove duplicate lines from a sorted file.

update Kernel daemon to flush dirty buffers back to disk.

uptime Display system uptime and average load.

userdel Delete a user account and related files.

V

vi(m) Start the vi (improved) editor.

vimtutor The Vim tutor.

vmstat Report virtual memory statistics.

W

w Show who is logged on and what they are doing.

wall Send a message to everybody's terminal.

wc Print the number of bytes, words and lines in files.

which Shows the full path of (shell) commands.

who Show who is logged on.

who am i Print effective user ID.

whois Query a whois or nicname database.

write Send a message to another user.

X

xauth X authority file utility.

xcdroast Graphical front end to cdrecord.

xclock Analog/digital clock for X.

xconsole Monitor system console messages with X.

xdm X Display Manager with support for XDMCP, host chooser.

xdvi DVI viewer.

xfs X font server.

xhost Server access control program for X

xinetd The extended Internet services daemon.

xload System load average display for X.

xlsfonts Server font list displayer for X.

xmms Audio player for X.

xpdf PDF viewer.

xterm Terminal emulator for X.

Z

zcat Compress or expand files.

zgrep Search possibly compressed files for a regular expression.

zmore Filter for viewing compressed text.

Index

195

E

echo 16, 22, 27, 122

editors 22

else 108

emacs 22

env 38

esac 114

escape characters 51

escape sequences 122

/etc/bashrc 33

/etc/passwd 2

/etc/profile 32

/etc/shells 2

exec 10, 132

execute permissions 23

execution 23

exit 114

exit status 105

expansion 12, 53

export 41

extended regular expressions 69

F

file descriptors 128, 131

file name expansion 53

find and replace 81

for 140

fork 10

functions 168

G

gawk 88

gawk commands 88

gawk fields 89

gawk formatting 90

gawk scripts 92

gawk variables 93

gedit 22

global variables 38

globbing 27

grep 69

H

here document 134

I

if 102

init 10, 17

initialization files 32

input field separator 42, 46, 93

interactive editing 79

interactive scripts 122

interactive shell 4, 4, 6

invocation 3

K

kill 176

killall 176

ksh (Korn shell) 2

Printed in the United Kingdom
by Lightning Source UK Ltd.
114959UKS00001B/204